TOO BUSY TO CLEAN?

TOO BUSY TO CLEAN?

Over 500 Tips & Techniques to Make Housecleaning Easier

PATTI BARRETT

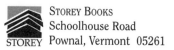

STOREY BOOKS
Schoolhouse Road
Pownal, Vermont 05261

*The mission of Storey Communications is to serve our customers
by publishing practical information that encourages personal
independence in harmony with the environment.*

Edited by Aimee Poirier and Pamela Lappies
Cover design by Jonathan Nix
Text design and production by Susan Bernier
Production assistance by Erin Lincourt and Eileen Clawson
Line drawings by Sue Storey
Indexed by Haggerty & Holloway

Printed in the United States

ISBN 1-56865-703-X

CONTENTS

✦ ✦ ✦ ✦ ✦

NOBODY'S PERFECT

"Excuse my dust."
— Dorothy Parker's suggestion
for her epitaph

Mention the word *housekeeping* to friends and watch what happens. Noses curl up; mouths turn into thin grimaces; talking ceases; eyes narrow. Housekeeping is associated with pain and drudgery. Rare is the person who at the mention of housework will smile and glow, remembering how she just finished polishing her copper pots to perfection.

Let's face it, housekeeping is a drag. We'd all like to be able to hire someone to do it. I spend lots of time wondering how I could afford to have live-in help, or at the very least someone to come in once a day to pick up everything that's strewn around the house, sweep the floor, gather up all the old newspapers, clean a window or two, and maybe, on special days, vacuum.

The unfortunate part about housework, in addition to the fact that it isn't fun, is that it's necessary. I guess most of us have been brought up to think it's proper to live in a seemingly tidy home. This doesn't mean that it must always be in great shape, but it should usually be fairly presentable. You need to be able to find things like the car keys and the important mail. It's always good to have a chair where someone can actually sit and some free space on a table where you can eat a sandwich or write a list of things that need to get done.

A fairly clean house makes you feel better about being in it; however, a too-clean house makes most of us feel nervous. That's when you start worrying about what you're eating and whether the kids are ruining something. No one likes to live like that. A house has to be a comfortable place to be.

My friends think I'm a lousy housekeeper. When they visit me they say hello and then start in cleaning the kitchen counter. They don't hold it against me, but I can tell they think I'm not very good at it. Not that my house is messy, really, but it does have its share of cobwebs hiding in places that don't bother me. I have a Zen attitude about killing those little bugs, and besides, who looks up at the ceiling? Not me, but some people do.

These same friends who comment on my collection of spiderwebs are the ones who check the silverware carefully before putting it into their mouths. It seems that once, a long, long time ago, one of them found dried cat food on her fork and since then has been reluctant to eat the delicious meals I dream up in my not-always-perfect kitchen. Maybe that's why my friends always ask for chopsticks now.

But I put up with their idiosyncrasies and don't even mind the fact that they insist on cleaning the counters until they're spotless. In fact, I rather enjoy it.

And, though I may not always clean my house to perfection, I have learned over the years many tricks about keeping the house clean — or at least making it *look* so. I collect tips the way some people collect baseball cards. You never know when you'll need a certain tip on how to clean brass or get a stain off the wall. In this book you'll find some of my favorite tips on how to make it easier on yourself and how to keep your house so it's easier to clean.

A LITTLE HISTORY

Why the emphasis on cleaning anyway? We tend to be influenced by the households in which we grew up. Keeping the house clean was important to my mother. She spent a good part of her life cleaning. Many of us who grew up in the suburbs in the '50s had moms like that: Our dads went to work and our moms cleaned. It wasn't that our house was very big, but boy you could sure clean it. Room by room, day by day. Lots of my friends' moms covered everything with plastic — that way you could really keep a room clean. Of course, you were never allowed in the room, but at least you knew it would be clean should someone come over to visit.

In a 1943 book called *Household Hints for Homemakers* by Eleanor Howe, the foreword speaks to the then-modern housewife:

"The making of a house a home is a woman's greatest objective. It is not a simple task, today or ever. For the busy homemaker must not only keep the house running smoothly, the family fed properly and clothed attractively, but she must also have time left to be a real wife and mother.

"Housekeeping — the means by which the running of a house is managed skillfully and efficiently — is chief among the tools with which such real homemaking is accomplished."

Thank heavens things have changed since then. The profile of the American household has changed, as have the characteristics of the people responsible for cleaning these households. More than 50 percent of American women work outside the home. This means there are more working wives and mothers and that more husbands and fathers are doing housework. More people live alone: Singles, of both sexes, face housework hassles, too.

Our goals have changed along with all of this. We may still like to have a tidy house, but it isn't our main objective. If our mothers wrinkle their noses as they run their fingers over the mantel, we just have to smile and accept our differences.

I think we've gone back in a way to our grandmother's or maybe our great-grandmother's day, when I don't think things were necessarily all that clean. Or at least not as clean as our poor mothers had to have things. Think about it: Before the vacuum cleaner arrived, women only had brooms and mops with which to clean. They didn't have to vacuum up every last bit of dust every day. And without electricity it was darker — you couldn't see the dirt! If you can't even see the dirt, how can it bother you?

The Israelites were among the cleanest early peoples. They incorporated strict rules for cleanliness, both personal and household, into religious law. One of the more drastic rules dictated by Moses stated that "If the house cannot be cleansed by scraping the walls and putting on fresh plaster, then the priest shall break down the house."

According to Homer, the Greeks also preferred a clean house, at least when expecting company. In the *Odyssey*, Ulysses' wife, Penelope, prepares to welcome guests by instructing her servants to "go busily and sweep the great hall, and sprinkle it — and others of you with sponges, wipe the tables clean."

It reminds me of the advice one dear elderly lady gave me when I asked her for her favorite cleaning tip. "Take your glasses off, dearie, just take your glasses off," she said as she smiled wisely.

So what have all these modern conveniences done for us? They've made us become more aware of how clean our house *can* be, and at the same time they've helped us become busier than we might *want* to be.

WHERE ARE WE NOW?

With a little bit of history behind us, and with the knowledge that we are just as busy today as our forebears were, we can proceed to tackle the problem before us. The first thing you have to do is decide just how clean your home needs to be. Once you have chosen your standard, you can decide just what you will have to do to maintain that desired level of cleanliness.

We may all be classified as one of the following: Some of us are real neatniks, other are absolute schlumps, and many others are something in between. Whatever you are, don't worry about it: You may be that way because of the way you were raised. Maybe your dad hounded you to be neat or you were punished as a toddler for getting dirt on a freshly painted wall. Current psychological theory holds that neatness traits come from modeling after parents and/or significant others. You either model your behavior after the one you were brought up with or you rebel. So if your mom is the kind who washes every bottle when she gets it back from the grocery store and wraps it in a plastic bag before putting it in the refrigerator, while you can't ever remember to put the cap on the dripping catsup bottle, much less wipe it off — don't worry, this is normal behavior. And it probably doesn't have anything to do with toilet training.

Even diehard neatniks can suffer from housework burnout, however. The nature of housework contains three of burnout's major stress components: It is repetitious, never ending, and extraordinarily low on positive feedback. In other words, the job is never done. There's always more to do.

I feel it and so do my friends: You're unappreciated. No one, least of all your kids, appreciates the time and effort that went into cleaning up a closet. Who can you grieve to? Cleaning is tough, and no matter how tough it is, it still has to get done. This book won't make it disappear, but with some luck it might help make it all feel a bit easier.

Who Does the Housework?

Despite the fact that most women are working outside the home today, it's clear that most are still taking responsibility for the bulk of the housecleaning in their homes, according to a survey conducted by the Johnson Wax Company.

The 1988 survey of 1,400 homes across America revealed that female heads of household devoted 11.2 hours per week to housecleaning, while male heads of household averaged just 3.9 hours per week. The overall average was 9.1 hours per week for both cleaning and cooking.

Among children, too, some sex differentiation occurs. Girls under eighteen spent 2.7 hours per week on household chores, and boys 2.0 hours per week.

The chores performed most often were tidying the house, taking out the trash, laundry, sweeping and vacuuming, and cleaning the bathroom.

Chores enjoyed most were tidying the house and grocery shopping (43 percent) and doing laundry (41 percent). Chores enjoyed least were cleaning the oven (48 percent), washing windows (44 percent), washing walls (43 percent), and ironing clothes (40 percent).

According to the chart below, you would have to iron for one hour — standing up — to work off a hamburger. An order of fries? Scrub the floor for an hour. Making beds for a steady hour will work off a light sandwich. At this rate, you'll never get skinny.

EXPENDITURE OF CALORIC ENERGY PER HOUR FOR HOUSEHOLD TASKS

Bed making	234
Sweeping	102
Preparing a meal	198
Scrubbing floors	216
Ironing, standing up	252
Running, 6 mi./hour	600
Fast dancing	400
Racquetball	800

— From *Nutrition Almanac,* Kirschman, 1984

Are You a Neatnik?

Have you ever heard yourself say the following?

◆ Who cares what the shrink says! I love having a clean home.
◆ I would rather live with Frankenstein than share my home with a slob.
◆ I just love having clean laundry around.
◆ Nothing makes me happier than having a neat desk and closet.

Or a Schlump?

- ◆ I don't attack the mess until it attacks me.
- ◆ Dirt? I don't see any dirt.
- ◆ Those aren't cobwebs, they're spiders' homes.
- ◆ Cleaning is a dirty job, but someone has to do it.
  Someone else.

Are you a neatnik? . . . Or a schlump?

2

EQUIPMENT: TOOLS FOR FIGHTING THE WAR ON DIRT

"If the only tool you have is a hammer, you tend to see every problem as a nail."

— Abraham Maslow

If you don't have the right stuff, you can't do the job right. Or, as my cleaning lady says, "I have to have my rags, my mop, and my broom or I can't do the job."

Thus, I rush out to buy clean diapers for rags and the best cotton mop I can find. Buying the best cleaning equipment is wise, as it lasts longer and usually works better, too.

VACUUM CLEANER

This is a must. If you are getting married, put one of these at the top of your wish list. A good canister-type vacuum can cost lots of money, so it makes a good wedding gift. Get one with the power drive in the beater head (this may be another attachment). The power drive has its own motor so you can get two motors working on one machine to get things really clean. The hose separates so it can be used for other tasks.

Buy from a dealer you trust. It's fine to buy from someone who comes to the door. Electrolux and Kirby, both excellent machines, are sold this way. The salesperson usually comes in and demonstrates the machine. Just be careful: One time a salesman vacuumed my rug for about thirty seconds and then emptied what he had picked up in that time — a mountain of dirt. Of course, it didn't occur to me until later that the dirt had been in the machine from the start.

If you have a two-story house you may want a heavy-duty vacuum cleaner for downstairs and a lighter one for upstairs, where there isn't so much heavy dirt accumulation.

A portable vacuum cleaner is important if you want to work with someone else and you each want your own vacuum. Those small, handheld vacuums, like the Dust-buster, are great, too. They plug into a wall-mounted unit that charges them continuously. Take them out when you need them for use in places like the car, or where the cat always likes to sleep, or when a visiting child drops cookies and Cheerios all over the floor. These are worth having for the convenience if nothing else — you don't have to drag out the vacuum and then be tripping over it for two days until you get around to putting it back. Some people have two, which might be obsessive behavior, but it can be handy to have one in the garage or shop and one near the kitchen. Great if you have a toddler around.

Take care of your vacuum. Read the manual carefully and follow its instructions. Don't run the vacuum cleaner over the cord, as a damaged cord can lead to shocks or fire. Avoid using extension cords and do try to use a standard wall outlet. Disconnect your vacuum cleaner from the outlet before changing bags, filters, brushes, or belts. Store the vacuum in a cool, dry area.

MOPS

I like a sponge mop. It's important to buy a good one so you can really clean into it without having it falling apart. Make sure you get one with a replaceable sponge. Chances are that at one time or another either you have bought a sponge mop only to find that the sponge has been permanently glued to the handle, or you have bought a replacement sponge later that won't fit your mop. This is a drag. When buying a sponge mop, I check to be sure the sponge isn't permanent and buy two replacements at the same time. This saves incredible headaches and guarantees that the whole unit will last much longer.

Some people swear by the wet mops with the cotton heads. These are okay, but I never have figured out how to use them, and when they get dirty they look really awful. If you use them dry, though, they're handy for dusting floors.

BROOMS

A well-made broom will be handy for those days when you don't feel like cleaning seriously. Then you can sweep. I am always amazed at all the junk that comes up when I sweep. People say if you sweep every day your house will be cleaner. I bet that's true.

Whisk brooms are ideal for cleaning things such as stairs, and for brushing things such as chairs and upholstered furniture.

Push brooms — with heavy-duty bristles and a thick handle — will clear away just about anything and are great for the basement and outdoor use.

A carpet sweeper is one of those old-fashioned things that still work well. Heavy-duty sweepers have double brushes and dustpans included, and you can wheel them right over your carpets without the noise or the cords.

> *"My favorite cleaning tool is a manual, hand-push carpet cleaner. You don't see them around much anymore but they are quick, convenient, effective, and quiet. For small, frequent jobs or when you want to clean when the baby is sleeping, they're great."*
>
> — Tip from a friend

FEATHER DUSTERS

Feather dusters are fabulous creations. Not only do they whisk the dust away but they are also fun to flit around. I have two — one upstairs in the bedroom and one in the hall downstairs stuck in a big urn filled with canes and umbrellas. Whenever I get the urge, I grab one and dust away. Get a long-handled one for those hard-to-reach cobwebs. I got mine from the Williams-Sonoma catalog, and it has a telescoping handle that extends to six feet. It's great for cobwebs in the stair-well and delicate china perched on high shelves.

"The lamb's-wool duster with a long handle is my favorite. You end up dusting and cleaning things you never touch — baseboards, tops of doors, picture frames, behind beds. And if you sing along when you use it, it feels great."

— Tip from a friend

BRUSHES

When scrubbing and scouring are necessary, brushes will do the job. Always buy good ones with stiff bristles.

A toilet brush is a must. Buy one for each bathroom. Some people like to store them in a plastic caddy by the john, but the brushes aren't very good and those caddies can be unattractive. I prefer hiding these brushes in a cabinet somewhere or placing them in an attractive basket. Avoid the brushes that have the bristles held in place with a twisted wire: They'll fall apart.

Tile brushes are large and handheld, with synthetic bristles that are great for scrubbing out the gook that gets in the grout between shower and tub tiles. They also work well in sinks and tubs.

Toothbrushes. Everyone knows that old toothbrushes are great for the small jobs that can't be reached otherwise. Try them around the knobs of your toilet seat (didn't know these had to be cleaned, did you?) or around the faucets. Great little items. If you don't have an old one, buy a new one.

Catalogs. If you like brushes for cleaning, don't be without the Fuller Brush catalog. When I was growing up, the Fuller Brush man used to come to our door and we always ended up buying something. Maybe that was why my mom's house was so clean. Its mail-order catalog is filled with brushes for every use. One set comes with a broom, a mop, and a long-handled scrub brush that can even get at grease. Another brush cleans the coils on your refrigerator. And there's even a brush designed to clean your coffeemaker. This is a fabulous catalog. Contact the Fuller Brush Company at P.O. Box 729, Great Bend, KS 67530; (316) 792-1711.

CLEANING CLOTHS

Some people call these rags, but they need not be. In fact, there are certain materials that you should not use. Cotton is good. Cloth diapers are great, if you can still find them, and so are men's underwear and old flannel nightgowns. Old linen napkins are wonderful, but with a new interest in old linens these are becoming pricey at tag sales and shops. Throw out those made from synthetic fibers — they won't hold up well and they don't absorb moisture or pick up dirt well.

If you are stuck on paper towels, buy good ones. The cheap ones aren't worth the money you think you are saving. Those Handiwipes you can buy work well because they rinse out easily and can be reused. Don't use newspaper for cleaning — it will make a real mess.

SPONGES

Sponges are indispensable. You'll need a few. Get some big ones and some of those sponges with a white nylon scrub pad on one side and a sponge on the other. The kind with a green scrub pad on one side and a sponge on the other is good for tough cleaning jobs like the oven.

Throw out sponges when they begin to shred at the edges or start to smell.

OTHER TOOLS

Buckets with double compartments are good because they hold both your cleaning solution and the rinse water. You will probably need more than one bucket: one for floors, one for washing the car, one for carrying flowers, and one for washing the dog.

Use **rubber gloves** when you work with cleaning solutions. Get good ones that won't fall apart.

Window squeegees hasten the job of cleaning windows. If you don't have one, an old windshield wiper will work.

"The greatest tool ever invented for cleaning — the Walkman."

— Tip from a friend

The right cleaning equipment can make you feel invincible.

CLEANING AGENTS

All-purpose cleaners. Heavy-duty liquid cleaners (Formula 409, Fantastik, and so on) and other spray-on cleaners are great for spray-and-wipe work such as cleaning counters and appliances of all kinds.

Ammonia. Clear ammonia is best because it works well on many surfaces. It acts as a good grease cutter, wax stripper, and soil remover. Also good for floors that are not suited to a polisher type of cleaner. A half cup in a gallon of water washes windows well. And to make oven cleaning easier, simply set a saucer of ammonia inside a cool oven overnight, then wipe out and clean as usual. (This is not for self-cleaning ovens, which could be damaged by such treatment.)

Baking soda. Now that we all have a box of baking soda hidden in the recesses of our refrigerator, we should also keep a few boxes handy for *all* those cleaning jobs that it works its wonders on. Baking soda can be used as a mild scouring powder that won't scratch or it can be mixed with water to create a paste for cleaning really dirty surfaces. It even deodorizes.

Bleach. Great for scrubbing out mildew in the bathroom and cleaning toilets, bleach can be used in many

WARNING!

Do not ever combine cleaning agents! Mixing products can cause chemical reactions that are harmful or deadly. For example, when bleach and ammonia are mixed they produce fumes that have killed people.

ways, but be careful as it is very strong. Wear rubber gloves. Don't breathe it for any length of time, and never mix it with ammonia or any ammonia-based products. It may cause fumes that can be deadly. Be sure the room you are working in is well ventilated. Bleach will get out the spot that nothing else will.

Lemon juice. Good for lightening ivory and cleaning ivory piano keys. Use lemon peels to deodorize your garbage disposal by grinding them with lots of water.

Light-duty liquid cleaners. Products such as Windex, for example, are used for mirrors and glass.

Scouring powders. These are must-haves. There are heavy-duty varieties such as Zud for rust spots in cast-iron tubs; basic cleaners such as Ajax and Comet or Bon Ami (a gentler, nonsilica powder) for sinks, bathtubs, and the like; and soft-scrub agents for use on fiberglass bathroom units, Formica countertops, and stainless-steel kitchen appliances. Buy what smells best to you.

Vinegar. Vinegar is as good a stain remover today as it was in Victorian times. One teaspoon of white vinegar in a quart of cold water will remove clothing stains when baby (or Dad) spits up. It also removes stains like coffee from good china.

Waxes, polishes, and oils. Used to shine and protect wood, leather, brass, silver, and other surfaces. Murphy's Oil Soap is a must for anyone with any wood in their home. It is great on wood floors and furniture. There are all kinds of polishes and oils to use. Some polishes you may need: silver polish and copper polish. Read the directions carefully and use only on recommended surfaces.

STORAGE

Where to keep all these cleaning supplies?

You really need a closet to store all the brooms and mops, or if you like to see everything — maybe as a reminder that the job needs to get done — hang them artistically on the wall of the laundry room in a kind of modern art collage. But if you are like me, you would sooner throw the buckets and sponge mops behind a door and forget they exist when you're not using them. Those divided containers you can buy in the house-wares section of the department store are great for bottles of cleaners and cloths and sponges and all. If you are organized you get one (or better yet, two) of these and put all your cleaning supplies in it. Keep one under the kitchen sink and maybe another in the upstairs bathroom. Grab it when you feel the urge to clean and you'll be able to whip around the house with everything at your fingertips.

Keeping Equipment at Hand

Since you are never sure when the urge to clean something will attack, it's good to be prepared. Pregnant women have a big problem with this: They want to have things ready for the baby-to-be and are known to wake up in the middle of the night because they realize the windowsills may be dirty. If this should happen to you, whether you are pregnant or not, it is much better to be ready for it. These divided containers are wonderful to have at the ready, no matter what your hormonal situation may be.

What should go in it? I have a plastic divided container and a more attractive basket-type one. The basket-type container is under the bathroom sink. (Just imagine your guests going to the bathroom and opening the door under the sink to check it out. Confess — don't you do that, too?) In your carryall you may put:

- All-purpose cleanser, like Ajax or Comet
- Liquid window cleaner like Windex
- A bottle of Fantastik or Formula 409 (spray is best)
- One white scrub pad/sponge combination
- One plain sponge
- A floor cleaner (like Mop and Glo)
- A bottle of ammonia
- Cleaning cloths
- Rubber gloves
- A toothbrush
- A paint scraper and a razor-blade holder with a sharp blade

Just think what you could clean with all of that stuff. If you have just such a well-equipped cleaning basket and can lug around your vacuum and your sponge mop, you are set. I sometimes like to leave it out on the kitchen counter because it looks so efficient. That way if someone comes over to visit they can see how you were just getting ready to clean the place.

3

GET IT TOGETHER! ORGANIZING YOURSELF

"If you want something done, ask a busy person."
— Benjamin Franklin

"Get it together!"

How many times have you heard those three words? Are people always telling you that? As though your whole life-problem would be solved if you could only "get it together." Getting it together is all about being organized — or seeing a shrink.

Some people are just born organized. They sail through life doing everything — job, house, family — and making it look easy. No problem. You look at them and you feel awful, wondering why you can't be like them. Why is it you can never find your keys when you need them, or that wonderful little serving bowl? And why can't you keep the week's mail all in one place?

Every once in a while I remember something that I own and I wonder where it is. It could be a sweater that all of a sudden I desperately need. I'll get up and turn the house upside down looking for it — tear the closets apart, scream at anyone who comes near me, and demand to know where my sweater is. Then, of course, I find it, tucked in the back of the sweater shelf. I breathe a sigh of relief and put it away again, realizing that I didn't need it after all, but panicked when I thought it had disappeared. This is not "together" behavior.

DEFINING YOUR NEEDS

My house is not terribly organized, but I always have plans to get it that way. I get on my biggest organizing kicks whenever I come back from visiting organized friends — the kind who have everything in its place. It amazes me. The kitchen is perfect. Bowls are neatly stacked. Spices are alphabetized. Pots and pans hang just so. There's always extra toilet paper and paper towels in the closet. Books are arranged by subject and author. It's beautiful and/or maddening.

I love being there, but when I come home I get depressed. I look around and realize that my house is comfortable, but it's not all that organized. My kitchen cabinets have a system that only I can understand, and sometimes it baffles even me.

Organizing yourself and your life really shouldn't be that hard. Using your time productively can make a big difference in your life. How you organize your time is a personal affair, really, and if you think that you are living the kind of life you want to you're probably right. But if you have the feeling that something has run amok — if you are frantic one day and lazy the next — then you may have to rethink how you use your time.

Are You Organized?

If you answer yes to all or many of these questions, you are in trouble and need to get organized:

1. Do you have trouble finding anything in your house in less than 20 minutes?
2. Have you ever lost a bill in that pile on your desk only to have your power turned off?
3. Do you forget appointments or birthdays?
4. Do things like glasses, gloves, and keys get misplaced easily?
5. Do you continue to think that all your storage problems would go away if only you had more room?
6. Do you refuse to use services that are out there to help you — cleaning people? baby-sitters?

LISTS TO KEEP

◆ Lists help with planning your day, as do day-by-day appointment calendars. You should at least keep a daily "to-do" list.

◆ Sometimes your lists of things to do can be divided among the members of your family. Give each child something to do. Your spouse and you may have already divided your chores.

◆ You may want to rank the to-dos in order of importance. If the lawn is two feet high and looks like it could stand a mowing, that would qualify as a number one priority, but the dust on top of the armoire can always wait a few more weeks. One good thing about dust is that it's always there.

How Lists Can Help

Lists can help you get organized in a number of ways:

◆ If you consolidate your downtown errands to one or two days a week, you will save time. Keep a running list going throughout the week so you won't forget to go to the dry cleaner's when you run into town to buy duck feed.

◆ A list always helps me remember to stop at stores that have just what we need but have been doing without for a while. Things like glue, Scotch tape, typewriter ribbons, envelopes. Jot it down when you think of it.

◆ Grouping tasks is important. It's like list making, really. When you take out the trash, think about emptying all the wastebaskets in the house, grabbing the piles of newspapers and catalogs while you're at it. Do laundry in large bunches rather than small ones, or have everyone do their own laundry. Thinking in lists will get you to combine similar tasks that can be accomplished in less time and with less effort when grouped together.

How Lists Can Hinder

Sometimes lists can be more trouble than they're worth. For example, if you are a new mother at home with your baby and are accustomed to getting a lot done each day, you'll only make it worse for yourself if you put down ten items on your daily list. Just put down one or two. It's difficult to get anything done when you have a baby because he or she may decide not to sleep and just want to gaze at your face all day. Believe me, don't think that spending the entire day holding your baby and crooning songs to him or her isn't a day well spent: You are giving that baby a good start in life. Forget your list. Forget your house. Order a pizza for dinner. Before you know it that baby will be a gawky teenager and you'll only have your memories of his or her infancy. But they'll be good ones.

In Peg Bracken's *I Hate to Housekeep Book* she offers this idea, called "Play Time-Planner's Russian Roulette." On separate slips of paper write down some of the unpleasant chores you have been putting off — clean the oven, reorganize file cabinet, balance checkbook — and, to make the game more fun, add some things you like to do — go for a walk, read a book, leave work early. Arrange these in a three-to-one ratio of pain to pleasure. Put the papers in an empty jar, and on a day when you can take the time, draw one. Even if you draw a horrible job, gambler's honor will get you started, and there's always hope for next time.

MANAGING TIME

Of course, how you handle the time you have is also important. If you can do something with those five minutes before you have to leave for work, so much the better. Maybe they could be spent watering the plants. Or if you can, do two things at once. This isn't so hard. Exercise or iron while watching television. Polish silver while talking with the kids or helping with homework.

Biorhythms

Biorhythms aren't totally New Age hoopla. They have been used to determine personal energy levels for a while now, and we are all influenced by them, whether or not we label them biorhythms.

Each of us experiences different energy levels at different times of the day. I know I'm a morning person — I can get lots more done in the morning than at night. I can't do anything after 9 P.M., and I know that 1 P.M. is my slow time of day. Thus, I schedule things accordingly. I iron in the morning. I get up and write in the morning before I go to work. Sometimes I make dinner in the morning.

If you are not aware of your own biorhythms, you may want to begin to pay more attention to your body and how you feel during the day. Try exercising in the morning and again in the afternoon. If you're exhausted after the afternoon workout you may be more of a morning person. Draw up a plan of your high- and low-energy times. After you know when you function best you can figure out when to do what. Plan your house-cleaning chores with this in mind. Since you will probably only do housekeeping part time anyway, do those high-energy jobs, such as vacuuming, sweeping, laundry, and ironing, when you know you'll have lots of energy. Vacuum in the morning if you are more awake then. It will help make the job go faster.

DOING TWO THINGS AT ONCE

Talk on the phone	Dust; wash dishes
Watch the soaps	Iron
Cook dinner	Clean fronts of cabinets
Do laundry	Iron
Do laundry	Read a book
Listen to opera	Wash windows
Do laundry	Polish silver
Do laundry	Clean out freezer
Pay bills	Do laundry

CLUTTER

Clutter is part of life. It always seems to be there — at least in most of the homes we know. Maybe it's not present in the streamlined apartments shown in the decorating magazines, with all that low white furniture and just a vase of flowers for a decorative touch. But the normal house is a mass — and a mess — of things. There are gobs of newspapers and catalogs that come each day in the mail whether we want them or not; there are toys with innumerable parts that get lost all over the house; there are collectibles that we buy at flea markets; there are old tobacco tins that some smart person long ago got rid of but that decorate our homes today.

Memories play a big part in the level of clutter in your life: pictures; scrapbooks filled with photographs; old papers from college and even high school; letters from friends whose faces you can't remember; records

In many cases, the solution is simply to organize the clutter.

that are warped but that have "your" song on them; knitted sweaters you started but never got beyond the back; the tennis racket you won with; and the list goes on.

Organize the Clutter

Don Aslett, the clutter expert and author of *Clutter's Last Stand,* basically says to get rid of it. He argues that most clutter is junk that we don't need in our lives and offers a systematic approach to how to eliminate it.

This sounds good. And after reading Aslett's guide, I too tried to cut down on my clutter. I started throwing out jars rather than saving them, I threw out college textbooks I wouldn't use again, I went through my closet and gave away clothes I hadn't worn in two years. But my heart wasn't in it.

I guess I like clutter. I like having lots of stuff around me, things like books. I put my books in every room: in the family room, in the guest room, in the bathroom, in my bedroom, and in the office. I like looking at them and having them there to read in case the urge hits me.

Along with the books go the magazines, and this can get to be a real mess. So I have shelves in each room: floor-to-ceiling bookshelves filled with books mostly, but with enough room for all the little things I cherish — things like vases and small framed photographs and antique dolls and toys from my own childhood. These fit in well. Overflow goes in baskets on the floor. Magazines I can't bear to part with are stacked in large baskets so the whole thing looks rather good and I know where they are if I need them.

So the key is to *organize the clutter*. There are many ways to do this.

Closets

- ◆ Line one or more sides of a clothes closet with shelves.
- ◆ Convert a shallow closet into a cabinet by adding floor-to-ceiling shelves.
- ◆ Put an old chest of drawers into a closet for extra storage space.
- ◆ If you have a tall closet near the kitchen, install shelves up high for rarely used items such as the popcorn popper and ice cream maker.

Shelves

- ◆ Install adjustable shelves when you can.
- ◆ Don't waste shelf space with oversize items. Create smaller shelves in between for other items.
- ◆ Any gap is suitable for shelves. If there's an indentation in a room, add some shelves, even if they are narrow. These are great for toys or small items.
- ◆ If you have limited storage space, build shelves up high for the overflow.

Stuff

Every home needs a place to put all the stuff that seems to come out of pockets and pocketbooks and doesn't know where to go — things that shouldn't be thrown out, but that don't have a place to call their own. Maybe a few stamps, or the mail that doesn't belong to you, or that skate key you know you'll need someday. Our spot for this stuff is an old desk whose top lifts up and reveals a big space that's perfect for the phone book and all of the things I don't know where else to put. I clean it out once a year or so. Now, having just been cleaned, it contains a phone book, lots of old photographs, an old bell, a deck of cards, a cribbage board, and some pamphlets that go with appliances and the like.

A bowl by the door is good for these things. It can be a gorgeous porcelain creation set on a lovely table. Who would know you are putting junk in it? Or maybe it's a basket on a shelf in the kitchen. The trick is not to let the stuff stay in there forever. Once a week someone has to go through it and figure out what to do with it. Often it will be simple enough: If no one has missed it or needed it all week, you may be safe to throw it out, but maybe you could go through it at the dinner table once a week to be sure that someone's valuables won't be tossed. (This assumes that your family is organized enough to eat dinner together.)

Wastebaskets

You can't have too many. Buy lots of wastebaskets. Collect them. Put them in every room. Put one next to the chair that you sit in when you watch television. Then when you finish your Popsicle you'll be sure to throw out the stick. Make sure the kids' rooms have lots of wastebaskets. Someone has to remember to empty them, though — this can be the tricky part. Make it someone's chore to go around the house with a big plastic garbage bag and empty all the wastebaskets. This will alleviate buildup.

Wastebaskets make good wedding gifts. Don't laugh: My husband and I received two really lovely ones when we got married and I thought at the time that it was the dumbest thing going. Except eighteen years later, we still use the things. They are good sturdy ones, and they're so attractive that they actually add something to the room.

Baskets in the kitchen are best with a lid, especially if you have a dog or cat. Baskets in the bathroom are nice if they can be cleaned easily. The heavy-duty plastic kinds work well.

Boxes

Boxes are great. Go to the liquor store and get a few big boxes. Take them home. Put them in the middle of the room. Throw all the junk into them. Throw out the boxes.

ADVICE FROM FRIENDS

- "Put mail in one spot always. If it isn't bills or important mail, it's given two days to be claimed. Otherwise it goes to the great beyond."
- "Learn to get rid of those things that are so important but that you never seem to use. For example, I gave up my need for my teddy bear when I was four or five years old, but after five years of marriage, I only just got rid of Ted last weekend. (I'm still crushed.)"
- "Work in fifteen-minute blocks. Allow fifteen minutes at some point every day to put away, hang up, and so on. Stop after fifteen minutes — not long enough to be a chore, but enough time so that something will be accomplished. Don't feel guilty about not achieving a perfectly clean house."
- "Clutter? There's no solution. Moving every five years may help."
- Motto: "Don't put it down, put it away."
- "Confine magazines to baskets that are cleaned out every couple of months."
- "Never go upstairs or downstairs empty handed — an adaptation of a rule I learned while waitressing."
- "Help each other with all the chores. Don't make garbage his job and vacuuming hers. But if one of you tolerates cleaning the bathroom and the other doesn't, don't waste energy trying to convince each other to do the detestable duty.

Fighting over housework is dumb. There are better things to do."

♦ "Don't try to do laundry and cleaning at the same time. Why? 1) Stopping to run up and down stairs switching clothes from washer to dryer makes cleaning seem to take forever. 2) You'll miss the end of the dryer cycle and will thus increase the amount of ironing you'll have to do."

♦ From Donna Mattoon, a friend and a mother of four who works, too: "I hate clutter. It upsets me to look at it. In fact, I can't seem to do anything else significant if there is clutter obstructing my focus. The only way I know of to deal with it has been a gradual move to make storage areas work well, both for the kids and for me.

"There is a big basket for shoes right inside the back door, a small set of drawers for hats and mittens, and hooks for jackets and school bags. (This stuff used to land on kitchen counters, right at dinnertime.)

"In the family room, we built beautiful cabinets where all the baby's toys are stored. It is now simple to clear everything away in a matter of seconds. In the children's rooms we are constantly refining shelves and closets to make them easy and accessible for the kids.

"One thing that is finally taking hold in our house is having one established place for one particular item. For example, paper, pens, crayons, and paste used to be stashed away all over the place. Now all craft items are stored in one old schoolmaster's desk in the kitchen.

"I now find that I am less bothered by clutter, knowing there is a place to store it when the time comes to put the stuff away."

FILING

Filing is an important part of organization. My best find at a garage sale was a large four-drawer wooden file. It now holds our personal financial records, and there's a drawer for more fun things — travel articles and brochures, my children's artwork, and miscellaneous written work. This way I know where to start looking for something that I may need in a hurry, such as my passport the day before I have to get on the airplane.

If you don't have the space for a large filing cabinet, try some of those cardboard filing boxes you can buy at an office supply store, or those new portable files that can be wheeled around and hidden in a closet.

Some people are frightened of filing. They're afraid if they file it they may never find it again. This just isn't true: If you *don't* file it you may never see it again. The trick is to file the stuff you want to save in the right place.

For example, some headings you may want in your file cabinet might include LETTERS, or, better yet, PERSONAL LETTERS. (Some people still write letters and, since one day they may be a collector's item, I like to save them.)

Letters. If you get a lot of letters, you'll need more than one file. You may want to file the letters according to the year you received them — LETTERS, 1996, LETTERS, 1997, and so on. Or if you get lots of letters from a few special people, you could file them according to name: LETTERS, JOHN; LETTERS, FRANCEY.

Files. A file for everything important about the house is good to have. Put in here everything you may need. Really important documents should go into a safe deposit box at the bank.

Insurance is a good file to have. You may want two — one for the house and one for the car.

Pets. Keep a file for each pet with his medical records — they can be handy to have around.

Appliances. Keep a file on each appliance so you can find the sales slip or the guarantee information when something goes wrong.

Artwork. A file for each child's artwork that you cannot bear to throw out is a good idea.

Important files. You may need a few files for your income taxes — one for medical expenses, one for contributions, one for the miscellaneous stuff. And of course a file for all your checks and one for receipts is handy.

Clippings. If you clip the newspaper frequently, you'll want to organize the clippings. You may need files for travel articles, health articles, ideas or tips to remember, and maybe one on entertainment that would include restaurant reviews you want to test yourself someday.

Organization. Remember to keep the files in alphabetical order. This really helps once you've started lots of files and don't know where to start looking.

Once you are even a little bit organized, housecleaning will be all the easier for you because everything in your house will have a place where it belongs. So if it's not in its place, just put it there, and already your house will be neater. The first step, then, is to assign a spot to everything in your house. If you find you have too much stuff, you may want to do a clean-out and throw-out of everything you don't need.

4

MAKING IT A HABIT: ESTABLISHING ROUTINES

"A place for everything and everything in its place."
— Mrs. Isabella Beeton's *Book of Household Management* (1861)

Nobody has enough time these days, what with jobs and children and activities, so who has time for extras like cleaning the house? It seems that finding the time to clean and establishing efficient routines are all-important to the art of cleaning. If you can time everything just so, you have got it made. Of course, if you could time everything just so, you would never be pregnant in July, have insurance bills due right after Christmas, or have the in-laws come for a visit in the middle of your midlife crisis.

Cleaning doesn't have to be one of those things that has a life of its own, however. We can control the workload if we establish routines to keep us on top of things. Some tasks need to be done every day, some only once a week, some twice a month, and some once a year or only once every three years. If you can figure out what needs to be done when, you're more than halfway there.

DAILY CHORES

I know it's hard to believe, but there are some things you have to (well, not *have to,* probably will *want to*) do every day in order to keep on top of the way the house looks. If you think about it for a moment, you'll realize that there are already plenty of things you do every day without even realizing it. Here's a sampling.

Put things away. Tops on the list in daily cleaning is putting things in their proper place — every day, many times a day if necessary. Move dirty dishes from the table to the dishwasher, put coats in the closet, dirty clothes in the hamper, trash outside, toys away. Remember, it takes less time to put things where they belong and completely avoid the clutter problem!

Make beds. Some people don't feel this has to be done, others do. Getting into a neat-looking bed is a wonderful feeling. Those duvets (comforters) that have washable covers are great for the easiest possible bed making. Simply tuck in the sheets, arrange the pillows, throw the duvet over the bed, and you've got it. Highly recommended for children.

"You can either close the bed or make the bed. Closing the bed means just throwing the covers back toward the headboard, which is okay by most people. Making the bed means hospital corners, puffed pillows, the works."

Do the dishes. Here, too, some people don't do dishes every day. Unless you're young and foolish, you have come to realize that avoiding the dishes just doesn't work. Dishwashers are fabulous — just be careful that they don't get clogged with too much gunk. Remember that a dirty kitchen filled with dirty dishes can affect the way others feel about food and cooking. Cooking is fun, really, and much easier if the kitchen is neat.

Take out the trash. No question — you have to do this as soon as it reaches the top, which in most families happens daily.

Review mail, magazines, and catalogs. Throw out junk mail and file bills to be paid and letters to be answered.

Clean cat box (if you are crazy enough to have one).

Clean off kitchen counters and all appliances as needed, with soap and water or a spray cleaner. If you run a damp sponge over these surfaces in the hope of cleaning them off, forget it — you're just spreading the grease around.

Wipe out bathroom and kitchen sinks after using them. In the bath I just use a dirty facecloth that then goes in the hamper; in the kitchen I take the last of the dish soap I have on the sponge or brush after doing the dinner dishes and swish it around.

Wipe off the toilet as needed.

Sweep floors as needed. If you sweep the kitchen and entry each day it will help matters. Get your child into this — sweeping can be fun. You will become mesmerized by the action and you actually can see progress being made.

Laundry. Some people do laundry every day. If you work and have a bunch of kids, doing a load on your way out the door might prevent piles from growing, but it will sit all day before it can be dried or hung out. It might be more efficient to make a concentrated laundry effort two or three days a week.

WEEKLY CHORES

The weekly chores are the meat and potatoes of your cleaning efforts. If you don't do certain things on a weekly basis you'll soon lose the battle and the war. Once a month isn't enough; twice a month isn't enough. You really have to tackle most cleaning jobs at least once a week.

One of many people's favorite jobs to do once a week — if they're lucky enough — is to write a check to the housekeeper. If this is one of your weekly chores, many of the other tasks mentioned hereafter will be unnecessary.

Vacuum. Yes, you have to vacuum every week. What did people do before the vacuum cleaner was invented? They relaxed. They had to do with brooms and sweepers what we now do with vacuum cleaners and electricity. Today there's no excuse for a grungy floor.

Frequent vacuuming prolongs the life of your carpet because it prevents a buildup of dirt that can cut carpet fibers.

You can cut cleaning time by putting thick mats or throw rugs at all the entrances to your house. These intercept and trap loose dirt, keeping it from being tracked into the house.

Dust and/or polish furniture. Remember: If you have mats at all your entrances it will cut down on cleaning time — and make dusting the first logical step in cleaning, since your floors and carpets will not release clouds of dust as you go around the house.

HOW TO CLEAN A ROOM QUICKLY

First, don't try to clean when you're dressed to kill. Avoid wearing decent clothes. Get into something baggy and comfortable. You can still wear makeup, though. People always seem to drop by for a visit just when you decide to really clean.

If you only have time to do one room — say you have thirty-five minutes to kill before you run your son to his baseball game — it's simple. First, carry all your appropriate cleaning supplies with you in your handy carryall.

Once in the room, take everything out of the room that doesn't belong there. Things that need to be cleaned separately, say a bowl or a vase, should go in one place to be cleaned in the kitchen. Do not put anything back until you have entirely cleaned the room.

Pull furniture out from the walls — unless it's too big and heavy, of course. Turn back the rugs at their edges and pick up small rugs to make vacuuming easier. Work your way around the room. Work from the top down. Dust away, vacuum furniture, wipe smudges off doorknobs, light switches, and walls.

Clean hard-surfaced floors next. Vacuum all hard floors with a brush attachment to avoid scratches. Straighten out rugs. Vacuum rugs more slowly.

Replace the furniture, dust the little stuff and replace it, and *voilà*, there's a fairly clean room. Don't worry about polishing or washing windows or scrubbing the floors — that's for another time.

Dusting is more than flitting around the house with a cloth or feather duster, singing as you go. It means scraping dirt off windowsills, removing all the dust from the living room furniture, and so on. I deal more with the how-tos of dusting in chapter 5.

Clean kitchen and other tile floors. Sweep, mop, and sponge with a sponge mop. See the sections on kitchen floors, page 70, and bathroom floors, page 78, of chapter 6.

Clean mirrors. (At least those you use often, such as those in the bathroom.)

Do laundry. See chapter 8 on laundry for this favorite activity.

Empty wastebaskets. It is easiest to take a big plastic garbage bag and run around the house emptying all the trash into it. This is a good job for a ten-year-old (or even younger) child.

Flip seat cushions in sofas and chairs.

Change bed linens. If you have the time, hang them outside instead of drying them in the dryer so they'll smell wonderful.

Iron. Didn't you just hate it when polyesters were out and cottons and linens were in again? Granted, they are wonderful fabrics and feel better on the skin, but they do need to be ironed carefully. Some people put their shirts in the refrigerator overnight before ironing them. I marvel at this. If I put my shirt in the refrigerator I would forget I owned it and it would never get ironed. Set up your ironing board in front of the television news and do two things at once.

Discard old newspapers, magazines, and catalogs.

Water houseplants. Sometimes this has to be done more than once a week. Too often is too much, I say. That's why I only grow succulents and cacti and those kinds of plants that can survive being watered just once a week. Group your plants in one spot to make it all the easier.

ANNUAL TASKS

Wash curtains, blinds, and shades. This is awesome work, really. I clean my blinds by taking them off the window and laying them in a tub of sudsy ammonia, then hanging them over the tub to dry. It is a lot of work, but it's not that difficult.

You can clean a window shade with a rough flannel cloth that has been dipped in flour. I know it sounds odd, but it works. A soft eraser will remove spots from shades. Keep parchment shades clean (if you happen to have any) by waxing them. Repair window shade tears with colorless nail polish.

Wash all windows (unless you believe in never washing windows). I have a few windows that I never wash because no one really looks out of them and they are usually covered by wooden interior shutters — why bother? Of course, I have to clean the shutters, and that is worse than cleaning windows, but no matter.

Screens have to be cleaned, too. Rub a brush-type roller lightly over the screen and see how easily it will pick up the dust. Or take the screen outside and wash it with your garden hose.

See chapter 5 for more information on window cleaning.

Go through clothes. Give away what you haven't worn in a year. Or if you think it's a priceless item, store it away in a proper place.

Vacuum radiators and heat ducts. This will help keep your heating system working efficiently The same goes for air conditioners.

Repot plants if they need it. Do this outside unless you have a spot for it in the house.

Clean barbecue grill and grate. Here's one to try: When coals have nearly reached their hottest point, tear off a sheet of heavy-duty aluminum foil large enough to completely cover the grill. Press the foil shiny-side down on the grill and fold the sides under, covering as tightly as you can. Place the grill over the

---

✕ LETTER FROM A YOUNG MAN ✕

"Sophomore year in college, when I acquired three roommates, was also the time I first learned the rules of housekeeping. Rule Number One is to ignore something long enough with the hope that somebody else will do it. Unfortunately, all four of us were good at this. After two months of ignoring the bathroom, I learned it would probably be more disgusting not to clean the toilet than to bite the bullet and take a sponge and bottle of ammonia in hand. This was the turning point in my housecleaning life.

"Now that I live alone, I find I straighten up when the spirit moves me or when someone is coming over. I do know dishes smell after a few days. Keeping junk off the kitchen table and a clean bathroom can make you feel everything looks good. Be sure to have an apartment with doors you can close. This helps."

coals for ten minutes. Remove foil, and any charred grease or food on the grill will drop off.

Wash or dry-clean bedspreads, slipcovers, and blankets.

Vacuum rug pads and the backs of rugs. I have to admit I have never done this, but my friend in the South says it is a must, and I trust her judgment.

Shampoo carpets; turn rugs to equalize wear.

Clean out garage, workshop, basement, attic. See chapter 7 for hints on cleaning these areas.

SEASONAL CLEANING

Seasoning cleaning is a leftover from another generation when everyone did "spring" and "fall" cleaning faithfully. This was big-time cleaning, when you did all the heavy work that you didn't get to the rest of the year. Windows, draperies, closets, garages, and attics were all part of this semiannual blitz.

It still is a good idea, of course, if you have the time. But really, if I did a spring cleaning, I'd have to take a vacation to do it, and who wants to waste vacation time on cleaning the house? Not me. So most of us fit the big stuff in and around our regular cleaning schedules.

One of the few seasonal tasks that people still do at least twice a year is to sort clothes. Lots of folks take

"Entertain once a month. That way your house will always be clean."

— Tip from a friend

the winter clothes to the dry cleaner in the early spring for storage throughout the warmer months. This works well but can be expensive. If you have children you'll be moving clothes around and cleaning closets and drawers when you change seasonal clothes. Be smart when you do this: If you have clothes you know your youngest child won't wear, give them to someone else with the same-size youngster. It's silly to keep clothes that won't be worn.

THE WHITE TORNADO: STRAIGHTENING UP FOR UNEXPECTED COMPANY

The phone rings. It's your long-lost roommate from college who just happens to be in the area. She'll be over in ten minutes, even though you told her to go the long way around town. The house is a mess. Try this:

1. Gather everything that is lying where it doesn't belong in the entryway and living area and throw it into an empty basket or bag. Hide filled basket.
2. Stack magazines and newspapers in an orderly pile. Plump up pillows on sofas.
3. Give the bathroom sink and toilet a quick rub. Straighten up the bathroom that she'll visit. Throw odds and ends in cabinets. If you have the time, put some Lysol on a rag and swish it around the sink a few times. This way the room will smell clean even if it really isn't.
4. Rinse any dishes and stack them neatly in the sink or in the dishwasher. Wipe counters.
5. Close doors to any room you don't want to display.

Sticking to routines can help you avoid "quick-clean" distress.

Another tip: Flowers do wonders. If it's summer and your house is a real disaster, pick a bunch of garden or roadside flowers and put them in a large vase or pitcher. The more flowers you have around, the less people will notice what is not in the best shape. The only trouble with flower arrangements is that they die. Throw out wilted arrangements and replace them with fresh ones in good order.

Dried arrangements are good because they last a long time, but they are not meant to last forever. After a year, throw them out, no matter how difficult it is. They are impossible to dust, and you can't wash a dried flower arrangement or it will fall apart.

Figure out what makes a room look clean. For some people a clean room means not having anything on the top of the refrigerator; for others it's having an uncluttered counter or nothing on the stairway. Some people think the house is great if the beds are made or the newspaper isn't on the floor. Learn what makes you, and the other members of the family, happy with your home. If your wife hates to come home from work and see debris piled around the kitchen, get the kids to pile it in the playroom. You'll be amazed at the difference.

✦ ✦ ✦ 5 ✦ ✦ ✦

PROCESS & PROCEDURE: THE HOW-TO OF IT ALL

"The wrongdoer is often the person who has left something undone rather than the person who has done something."
— Marcus Aurelius (2nd century A.D.)

"Process and procedure" is a fancy way of labeling what cleaning is all about. It's the real "how-to" of what you have to do. Today you really have to know *how* to vacuum. It doesn't take all that much know-how, really, but if you think about what you're doing before you tackle the job, it will be all the easier.

It's really a matter of being organized. If you are an organized person, you know that it makes more sense to dust before you vacuum. If you clean with your roommate, one of you should be the duster and the other should follow around with the vac. That's organization. If you have to do it yourself grab a cloth and dust the room down first before you vacuum. Do one room at a time and be thorough. That kind of planning can really help lighten the load.

An essential part of cleaning is planning your strategy. A few moments spent contemplating how best to go about cleaning your house will really help things in the end. You may even want to draw a map of your house before you start, and figure out where to start and finish. This way you won't backtrack and lose valuable time.

DUSTING

Dusting isn't really too complicated, but it does involve a bit more than just moving the dust around and letting it fly around as you blow through a room. Most of us probably got our start in housecleaning by dusting. Our mothers would give us an old diaper and tell us to dust the living room, and it would be fun: We could draw in the dust and then erase it just like a blackboard.

But as much as I have fond memories of dusting, I've fixed it so that I have very little to dust in my house. Every piece of furniture with a flat surface is so covered with stuff that the dust is hard to see. Or else the surface is rough and doesn't show the dust. If you decide to decorate your house with primitive American pieces, which are mostly painted wood, you'll find that the dust doesn't show like it does on polished surfaces. Great stuff. Of course, dust still manages to land on other things, so I haven't been able to avoid it completely.

"Dusting makes you feel like you have a clean house even if you don't."
— Erik Bruun, a single male housekeeper

When you go dusting, take these items with you:

◆ Dust rags or cleaning cloths (cotton)
◆ Feather duster
◆ Bottle of dusting spray
◆ Whisk broom
◆ Furniture polish
◆ Toothbrush

Work from high to low (dust falls down). Check the ceiling first and then work your way down. Check for cobwebs (forget that it may be Charlotte spinning her web). Concentrate on one area at a time and dust it completely before you move on. Don't dust a whole room and then go around and polish or return to dust some more.

Using the Feather Duster

Don't flick your wrist and let feathers flip into the air because the dust will hit the air again, too, negating all the work you just did. You want the dust on the floor. So every once in a while, hit the duster across your ankle to get the dust onto the floor.

Dusting Plan

1. Check for cobwebs.
2. Look for fingerprints at eye level and below. Wipe with cleaner.
3. Dust mirrors and pictures, especially the top and bottom of the frame where dust always lands.
4. Check walls for marks and clean off.
5. Dust the surface of tables as well as around and above. You don't have to use furniture polish each week. Remove tablecloths and take them outside to shake them out. Launder if necessary.

6. Dust items on tables, carefully. Either remove everything from the table and dust it separately or dust around the objects. Use two hands to move objects, and don't push them across the table — pick them up.

7. Use a whisk broom on the couch or other upholstered furniture.

8. Dust plants with the feather duster. Pick up dead leaves.

9. Dust windows — tops, sides, and sills.

10. Dust and clean the telephone.

11. Use the feather duster or a cloth to dust books sitting on the shelves. Once or twice a year give a thorough going-over on a rainy Saturday when you have nothing to do. This will help keep your books in good condition.

Things Not to Forget While Dusting

- Windowsills
- Light fixtures
- Crossbeams of tables
- Drawer pulls
- Shutters, venetian blinds, mini blinds, shades
- Baseboards
- Television tubes
- Heater vents
- Tops of drapes
- Backs of chairs and underneath chairs
- Computers

Plants

How to clean your favorite leafy green things is a question that comes up quite a bit. If you have a rubber tree in your living room, you know how dusty those big flat leaves can get. Wipe them with a cloth weekly if needed; a little water on the cloth is fine.

What to Dust It With

Item	Dust with
Blinds	Feather duster followed by soft cloth
CDs	Soft cloth
Computer	Wipe screen regularly with soft cloth
Couch	Vacuum
Glass-framed pictures	Cloth, liquid glass cleaner
Lampshades	Feather duster, brush attachment of vacuum cleaner
Oil paintings	Feather duster, very soft cloth
Radiator	Vacuum, feather duster
Records	Soft cloth
Screen	Sponge with dishwashing soap, rinse, buff dry
Shutters	Vacuum; wipe with damp sponge
Stereo	Soft cloth
Telephone	Cloth, rag with liquid cleaner
Television	Soft cloth; vacuum with small brush attachment
Woodstove	Enamel: Wipe and wash when cool Black: Reblack occasionally

Some people use mayonnaise on a cloth to make the leaves shiny. I don't buy that because I don't like to put anything on leaves other than water or maybe one of those special fertilizers that are fed to the plant through the leaves. Avoid shiny-leaf products. They're a lot of work and of questionable value.

Instead, put your plant out in the rain or in the shower once in a while, or give it a good hosing. If your plant is too big for that, it might be time to consider getting a new plant. If you like trees inside your house, you might just have to live with dusty trees. Some leaves are undustable: Spray water on them and learn to like it.

Books, Videocassettes, Compact Discs, Records

Books, videocassettes, compact discs, and records all need to be dusted and taken care of. First, store these things toward the edge of the shelf so air can get around them. Don't store them in direct sunlight as this will cause the books to fade and records to warp. You can dust or give a quick vacuum with the little brush attachment to all the books on the shelf. To really work at it, tilt each book backward and forward on the shelf so you can remove dust from bindings and edges.

Leather-bound books need to be treated once in a while with lightweight oil so that the leather won't dry and crack. Vinyl books can be washed with a mild detergent solution and then treated with a light coating of Vaseline jelly.

And here's a good one from a friend with a lot of books: Rub grease spots out of books with soft white-bread crumbs. Clean badly soiled edges of paper with a gum eraser. Be careful not to damage the pages while you do this.

VACUUMING

Vacuuming is amazing when you think about it. What else can accomplish so much with relatively so little effort? Just suck up all the dirt into that little bag and then throw the bag out.

Use two vacuum cleaners: a big canister-type vac for carpets and rugs and a smaller vac for hardwood floors, kitchen floors, and the like. The key to vacuuming is to have a system so you don't forget a spot and do an area more than once. If you are vacuuming a large wall-to-wall carpet, break it down into sections. Think of it like mowing the lawn. When you mow the lawn you go over it in neat rows — do the same with your rug: Divide the rug or floor into quarters, and vacuum that entire quarter before moving on to the next quarter.

Take your time, especially when you are working on a thick carpet. There's lots of dirt in there. One pass over the carpet is not enough — you'll have to go over each section several times. Work slowly so the suction will really pick up all that dirt. Go more slowly in well-used areas and faster in areas that see only light traffic.

Vacuum areas of heavy traffic frequently, maybe (and I know this sounds horrible) more than once a week. This means hallways, doorways to the kitchen, and areas around chairs where feet will grind all that dirt into the rug.

Rugs

Vacuum both the top and bottom of rugs to keep dirt from wearing out the fibers.

Natural fiber rugs. Rugs made of sisal or grass can be vacuumed and then treated with a damp cloth to keep moisture in.

Fur rugs. Work cornmeal through the pile until the cornmeal shakes out clean. Then vacuum up all that is left.

Washable rugs. Air-dry small rugs to keep their shape, or dry flat. Don't hang them to dry, or their shape may change.

Hard surfaces. It's always a good idea to vacuum hard-surfaced floors before you wash them. That way the dirt doesn't get ground into the floor with the mop — or, worse yet, turn into mud. Use the floor nozzle attachment that has a brush on it when you vacuum the floor so you won't scratch it. Go back and forth in two slow strokes to pick up the loose dirt. Put on the small brush attachment or that funny long one to clean around baseboards and under radiators.

> *"A few times a year you may have to take the cushions off the upholstered pieces and take them outside and beat them senseless. Unbelievable amounts of dust will come up — and you'll find all kinds of things under the cushions."*

Stairs

Vacuuming stairs is not much fun. If anyone tells you otherwise don't believe them. Start at the top and vacuum your way down. If you use a canister-type vac, set it on one of the steps below — about six from the top or so — and move it down as you go down. Be careful not to fall and land with the vacuum on top of you. Stairs have be vacuumed often because they usually get so much use.

Maneuvering Furniture

Move furniture when you vacuum. Remember to move it the shortest distance possible. Tip a chair back instead of carrying it out of the room. Pull the bed out from the wall to get to that horrible spot where all the dental floss and tissues go. This is almost as bad as cleaning out a drain.

Watch out for electrical cords on the floor as you vacuum, as these collect untold amounts of dust. Vacuum carefully around them.

Furniture needs vacuuming, too. Start at one side of a chair on the top and vacuum to the bottom, opposite side. This way you'll get the whole thing.

Stereo Equipment

Vacuum your record and compact disc collection often. Vacuum your stereo, too. If there's a lot of dust around the stylus on your stereo's turntable, clean it with a small paintbrush dipped in isopropyl alcohol. Dust records while they are on the turntable. Use a cleaner that's made for this and clean *with* the grooves, not against them.

CLEANING CLOSETS

If the closet isn't organized to begin with, it will never come clean. It's true. And with everything they sell today to organize closets — the shoe racks, the sweater shelves, the six-in-one hangers — almost any closet can be organized in a hurry.

To clean a closet you must first determine that closet's function. Decide what it will be by asking a few questions. Ask, "Where am I going when I pass this closet?" If it's between the dining area and kitchen and it is now filled with junk, you might do better to build shelves in it and store large china pieces and tablecloths. The closet in the hall near the bedroom may be good for linens. Remember that you want to store things near where they will be used.

Step by Step

1. Get lots of cardboard boxes and bags and begin by carefully sorting out the stuff in the closet. One box goes to the dump, another to the church bazaar, another to a different closet, and the rest will be rearranged in the closet you are cleaning.

2. Don't empty the whole closet at once. Go one section at a time, maybe two shelves one day and two the next. You don't want to get so exhausted that you give the whole thing up.

3. After you have gone through the closet and have your box of things that will stay, take a good look at the space and see if you need new shelves. If so, do it now before you put all the junk back or you'll never do it.

4. If you don't need any more shelves you might want to paint the closet. This will really give it a lift. Painting a closet will definitely make it look clean, or so I am told. I have never done it myself — the idea of doing all that work for something you can close the door on astounds me — but some people paint their closets and line the shelves with fancy paper. You may want to try it. Make it extra special

by using paper to match the wallpaper or the curtains or the bedspread. Throw in lots of sachets and you have what is known now as a "designer closet." If you have one of these, leave the door open.

5. Lights in closets are good and bad: good because they help you find things when you need them, bad because they also let you see the dirt.

WINDOWS

I love my Aunt Frances. Well, she's really my husband's Aunt Frances, but she has the same philosophy on cleaning that I do. For example, she never cleans windows. She doesn't believe in it. I think that's a fabulous idea, so now I never clean windows. Well, I do have an exception — a big picture window that I look through each morning to watch the birds. It keeps me sane

A little teamwork can make housecleaning more enjoyable.

throughout our long winters. This window I clean quite a bit. Maybe twice a year.

Some people do clean all their windows regularly, and they say that washing them twice a year is a good plan. One friend gets everyone in the family involved and they make it into a game, with kids and adults running all over trying to clean all the windows in a certain amount of time. Another good thing to do is to hire someone to do it.

Tips for Washing Windows

Use vertical strokes when washing outside and horizontal strokes when washing inside (or vice versa). This way you will know which side the streaks are on.

Wash windows from the top to the bottom so you won't have drips messing up what you have already done.

Use a long-handled squeegee on big windows. These are fun to use and don't leave many streaks.

If you want real shine, rub a clean blackboard eraser over a just-washed window and stand back!

Don't let window cleaner get on woodwork, as it can damage it. And never use steel wool on glass.

Try not to wash windows on the sunniest day of the week, as the glass may streak and it's better for your health to *enjoy* the sun.

What to use? Some say use newspaper. Others say use anything *but* newspaper. One friend says that newspaper crumbled up and dipped into a bowl filled with vinegar works wonders. She dips the paper, puts it on the window, and wipes the glass until it's almost dry with the same paper. Then she shines it with a cloth or more newspaper, dry this time.

Super Solutions

- Mix ⅓ cup ammonia in 1 gallon warm water. Apply with a sponge or pour into a spray bottle.
- On cold days add ½ cup rubbing alcohol to each quart of water used and you won't have any ice.
- Another solution: Add ½ cup ammonia, 1 cup white vinegar, and 2 tablespoons cornstarch to a bucket of warm water.
- Spotted sills: Pour diluted rubbing alcohol on a cloth and rub the entire sill. They'll look newly painted.
- Grease spots: Use leftover cola drink.
- The tracks of a sliding glass door: almost impossible. One friend wraps a cloth around an eraser and rubs away.
- Screen windows: Rub a brush-type roller over the screen and it will pick up dust.
- Use cream silver polish on aluminum window frames.
- Wear rubber gloves when you use any strong window cleaner.

WALLS

Yes, walls get dirty, too, even though they are vertical. Amazing, isn't it? Dirt is all around us even when we don't notice it.

Of course, walls get dirty when kids put their hands on them or when they decide to color on them — or worse. I've learned that if you don't deal with the dirt that builds up on the walls regularly, you'll be in real trouble when you go to deal with a spot. When trying to take off a spot, you often wind up with a lot of gook on the wall, usually in the form of a round, gray spot. Not fun.

So here's the thing: You can vacuum your walls. Isn't that wild? When they get bad you can use an all-purpose cleaner on the washable walls.

Wash walls from the bottom to the top. This can be a pain. Sometimes I prefer to just repaint the walls.

Remove tape from a wall with a warm iron. Through a protective cloth, press the tape with the iron to loosen its backing.

Rub finger smudges right away. (This is much easier said than done. I usually leave smudges for a few years as sentimental reminders of my kids' cute, chubby fingers.)

Clean brick walls with water and cleaner, and if the mortar is dirty, try some bleach. Smoke stains around a fireplace can be removed with an abrasive cleaner. Rinse well.

Painted Walls and Wallpaper

Walls that have been painted with latex-based paint are easy to wash after the paint has been on a while. Oil-based paint can be cleaned, too. Use a commercial all-purpose cleaner, or try one of the solutions below:

- ◆ Mix 1 cup ammonia, ½ cup vinegar, and ¼ cup baking soda with 1 gallon water. This is strong stuff — use your rubber gloves. Rinse well.
- ◆ Lighter fluid will take off crayon marks on walls. Put a little on a cloth and rub carefully.
- ◆ Alcohol works on those funny black spots on the wall. Test an area first, though.
- ◆ Be careful with wallpaper. Try to save the instructions that came with it. Some papers can be washed but many cannot.

- Erasers are handy for removing spots.
- Clean grease by blotting first with paper towels and sprinkling cornstarch on the stain. Rub off the cornstarch when it has soaked up the grease and vacuum.
- Chunks of soft, stale bread rubbed over wallpaper can erase soiled areas. I like rye.
- More grease? Put baby powder on a clean powder puff. Rub the puff over the spot until grease disappears.
- Use nylon stockings bunched up into a ball to clean rough plaster walls.

Wood Paneling

Be careful with wood paneling. I would only dust or vacuum it unless it has an oil finish — then you can use a commercial cleaner.

Hint: Rub mayonnaise into white water marks on wood paneling. Wipe it off twelve hours later. The marks should be gone.

CEILINGS

If you look up once in a while you will notice that your ceiling isn't as clean as it once was.

You can vacuum your ceiling or use your long-handled feather duster unless it's a very high ceiling, in which case the dirt is good and far away. Use a

---

"The best way to clean house is in the nude. Suddenly what was boring and dull becomes exciting."
— Tip from a friend

---

sponge mop on the ceiling if it is bad. Some ceiling tiles can be cleaned with an all-purpose cleaner. Most ceilings are painted — you can wash these easily with an all-purpose cleaner.

FIREPLACES

I have no idea why you would want to clean a fireplace unless you are planning a major event at your house where everything has to be cleaned just for the sake of it. I figure the burning that goes on in fireplaces keeps them clean enough, but sometimes in the summer when you are having a party and want to fill the fireplace with a big flower arrangement you may want to clean it out.

Vacuum the hearth regularly, but be extremely careful not to vacuum up any burning embers: This will ruin your vacuum cleaner to be sure. Inspect the firebox, flue, and chimney yearly for creosote buildup. You may want to have the chimney professionally cleaned to prevent chimney fires when too much creosote builds up.

Don't use an abrasive cleaner inside the fireplace. Many leave a flammable residue, and they can also wear away the firebrick.

Scrub the walls of the firebox opening with a stiff brush but, again, be careful not to harm the firebrick.

To clean glass fireplace enclosures, remove smoke stains with a solution of ½ cup vinegar in 1 gallon warm water. Add a tablespoon of ammonia. Spray on or wipe on with a cloth. Rinse and dry with a clean cloth.

Hearth and Mantel

Smoke stains around a fireplace can look ugly, especially when you're not using the fireplace for anything but a decorative element in the room. You can use abrasive cleanser on decorative brick — scrub the powder into the moistened brick and then rinse. If brick is really a mess, get a commercial brick cleaner and a stiff-bristled brush. If your hearth is made of ceramic tile, you may want to clean the grout occasionally with a toothbrush and a spray tile cleaner.

Don't use abrasives on a marble mantel; use a damp sponge. Borax rubbed into the marble with a wet cloth also works well.

HEATING UNITS

Gross. That's the only word for what goes on under and around your heating units. Look at all that junk that collects around those heaters. And if you don't keep them clean, all that dust will recirculate when you turn the heat on.

Vacuum cleaners are fabulous when it comes to heating units. Be sure to vacuum the heaters when you vacuum the floor. When they begin to look bad, wash the surfaces of baseboard units or radiators with an all-purpose cleaner.

✦ ✦ ✦ 6 ✦ ✦ ✦

KITCHENS & BATHROOMS: THE GRUESOME TWOSOME

"We are made as the filth of the world, and are the offscouring of all things unto this day."
— I Corinthians 4:13

Most rooms that we live in are pretty much the same: They have a floor, walls, a window or two, and a closet or storage space. All of these things need vacuuming, dusting, organizing — the whole bit. But there are two rooms that require special attention: the kitchen and the bathroom. These are the rooms that somehow always need to be cleaned. Always. You can't get away with not cleaning them unless you live alone and really don't care about what kind of place you live in. But most of us do have people in once in a while, and usually these people have to use the bathroom or want a cup of tea, so these two rooms demand a bit of extra attention.

Let's start with the kitchen.

THE KITCHEN

Kitchens are more than just kitchens nowadays. They are bright family rooms where everyone seems to gather after a day in the real world. More than cooking goes on here. Sometimes we put a desk, a computer, a television — maybe even a couch or an easy chair — in the kitchen, in addition to all the usual kitchen paraphernalia.

But even in the modern family-room type of kitchen, cooking still goes on, so this room is going to get extra messy. Eggs will break. Milk will spill. Dinners will be burned on top of the stove. The only way to control all of these disasters is to establish daily cleanup rules.

If everybody in the house works together at keeping the kitchen clean, the big jobs won't seem as awesome. And the big jobs will *tell* you when they have to be done. When your sneakers stick to the floor, it's time to wash the floor. When the refrigerator starts to smell, it's time to clean it out. And when the smoke alarms in the house go off every time you turn on the oven, it's time to clean that oven. You get the idea.

Counters and Cupboards

Start cleaning the cupboards first because they are higher up than almost anything else. Usually you just have to watch for the fingerprints on the handles. Counters always have to be cleaned. Work from back to front, being sure to move canisters, toasters, and so on, to clean underneath them. Use a toothbrush to clean around drawer or cabinet handles. Spray and wipe as you go.

Continue around the kitchen. Look for spiderwebs as you go. Dust these with the feather duster, or a long-handled brush for high spots.

Often the big jobs will *tell* you when they need to be done.

Open shelves can be dusted with the duster, too. To clean a shelf, move all the items to one side and clean the empty side, then move everything over to the side you've cleaned and repeat. If the shelf is too full, move just enough of the stuff to the counter so there's space to move what is left.

Cleaning Different Surface Materials

Acrylic. Use a mild abrasive liquid or a powdered cleanser applied directly on a wet surface. Rinse well and dry.

Ceramic tile. Clean grout with a toothbrush and a spray tile cleaner.

Plastic laminate. Use one of those two-sided sponges with fiber on one side and sponge on the other. The fiber is gentle but abrasive and will get out many stains. Use the sponge side to wipe the surface off. Baking soda works wonders on counters.

Wood. Once in a while, rub oil into the wood to protect it. Use a salad oil or a boiled linseed oil. Baking soda cleans and deodorizes wood surfaces. Mix ½ cup with 1 quart warm water. Rub into a paste on the wood, rinse well with clear water, and pat dry. When dry, restore by rubbing in salad oil or linseed oil with a very fine steel-wool pad. You can treat counters with two coats of oil, applied twenty-four hours apart.

Large Appliances

Refrigerator. Wipe the top off first, if you can. Maybe you just have to dust it, or maybe yours is like mine, with a cabinet over it so you can ignore it.

Wipe those fingerprints off the outside. Clean around the hinges and nameplate with a toothbrush. Open the door and clean off the rubber gasket. (This needs to be kept clean so the door will close well.)

Wipe the yucky air vent while the door is open, or use your duster or vacuum cleaner. Clean the spot where the gasket meets the surface on the inside of the refrigerator. All this should be done weekly.

Every once in a while, you have to give the refrigerator a big cleaning. Choose a time to clean when there's little food in the fridge and freezer. Turn it off earlier to defrost before you clean it.

Once ice is loose in the freezer, it's not too hard to clean. Put loose ice and ice trays in the sink. Remove the items inside and spray a cleaner in the freezer.

Remove the shelves and clean them in a mild, soapy solution. Dry thoroughly.

Inside the refrigerator, start by cleaning the shelves. If they are very bad, take them out and clean them in the sink; if not, they can be wiped where they are. Throw out anything old or gross as you clean — it really helps.

Remove drawers and bins and clean both inside and out. Clean under the bottom drawers, as that area is usually a mess. Be sure to check the drain pan if there is one and clean this out, too.

Stove. There are two basic types of stove tops: gas and electric. Gas stoves are easier to clean than electric. Remove the grills from the burners and spray and wipe the surface underneath. Sometimes you may have to use an abrasive cleanser and pad to take off gunk that sticks.

Electric stoves usually have a ring of chrome or aluminum around the burners that needs work. Sometimes a toothbrush can get around these; other times you will have to take the ring off to really get under the grime. The drip pans also need to be kept clean. These are very hard to keep looking good, though. Instead, buy new ones when they become dirty — it's so much easier.

Once the top is clean, work on the front. First, remove all control knobs and clean them in soapy water — then you can clean the surface.

Open the door and get the inside of the door window clean.

To clean the metal mesh filter that covers the fan above the stove, rinse off whatever grease you can and use a scrub brush to loosen what's left. Then put it in your dishwasher and let that do the work for you.

Oven. Cleaning the inside of the oven is the worst job in the world. I strongly advise you to buy a self-cleaning oven. These are worth their price, as they really do clean themselves. Fabulous. If you don't have one, prepare yourself for the worst. There are lots of products on the market for oven cleaning. They are all a bit hazardous, so be sure to wear rubber gloves. Avoid dripping oven cleaner onto any surface other than the oven. Always read the instructions carefully before using.

◆ Do wipe up spills from the self-cleaning or continuous-cleaning ovens so they won't burn and stain the inside surfaces.

◆ Sprinkle spills with salt. When the oven is cool, brush off burned food and wipe with a damp sponge.

◆ Sprinkle the bottom of the oven with automatic dishwasher soap and cover with wet paper towels. Let it stand a few hours, then wipe.

◆ Follow the instructions that come with the oven on how best to keep it clean.

Microwave. If you keep it clean, you'll never have to exert yourself. Wipe the exterior when you do the counters and wipe the inside after each use. Use a mild detergent, glass cleaner, or baking soda to clean stains. Never use a commercial oven cleaner.

Dishwasher. Dip a damp rag in baking soda and use it to clean spots inside and outside the dishwasher. A glass cleaner will clean chrome trim.

◆ If the inside smells a bit, sprinkle some baking soda in the bottom and allow it to sit overnight.

◆ Never put any silver, aluminum, or brass in the dishwasher.

◆ To remove film from dishes and from the dishwasher, put a bowl in the bottom of the washer and pour 1 cup bleach into it. Run through the washing cycle but *do not dry*. Then fill the bowl again with 1 cup white vinegar and let the dish-washer go through its entire cycle.

Clothes washer and dryer. These are usually kept hidden, but some people have them in the kitchen. Wipe exteriors with a damp cloth and clean with a liquid cleaner. Baking soda works well here, too.

Small Appliances

Toaster. Unplug the toaster before you clean it. Remove the crumb tray and shake out the crumbs. Wipe the exterior. Use a brush to get crumbs out of the inside. Shake out toasters that don't have a crumb tray.

Toaster oven. Try to clean this after each use. Wipe the outside regularly.

- A scouring pad will get out most dirt and stains from the tray.
- Clean only when it's cool and when it has been unplugged. Don't immerse this or any small appliance in water.
- Baking soda works well on toaster ovens to keep them shiny.
- A razor blade can be used on the inside glass of the oven door to take off the really bad stuff.

Food processor and blender. Read the booklet that comes with these for cleaning ideas.

- Clean bases with a good liquid cleaner. Glass cleaner can be used on stainless-steel bases of blenders. Spray on and buff dry.
- Fill the blender partway with hot water and a few drops of detergent. Cover and turn on for a few seconds. Rinse and drain dry.

Electric can opener. To clean the blades on your electric can opener, run a paper towel through the cutting process.

The Sink

You can't clean the sink unless it's empty — you should have already washed and put away the dishes. Sinks are relatively big tasks.

Clean the top with a liquid kitchen cleaner and use a toothbrush around the faucets and around the area where the sink meets the counter. Wipe clean and dry.

Use powdered cleanser inside the sink. Sprinkle a little on the bottom and use a pad to swish it around. Rinse thoroughly to get rid of all the cleanser.

For a sparkling white sink, place paper towels across the bottom and saturate with bleach. Let set for a half hour or so.

If the drain is clogged with grease pour a cup of salt and a cup of baking soda down the drain, followed by a kettle of boiling water. The grease will dissolve.

Remove rust marks by rubbing stainless-steel sinks with lighter fluid if rust marks appear. After rust disappears, wipe with liquid cleaner.

Remove water spots from stainless steel by using a cloth dampened with rubbing alcohol or white vinegar. Club soda or white vinegar will shine stainless steel fast.

Kitchen Floor

First you need to vacuum the floor to get up all the crud. Then it depends on the type of floor you have.

If your floor is no-wax vinyl, hardwood covered with polyurethane, or tile, fill a bucket or sink with a little ammonia and lots of water. Mop the floor with this, rinsing often. If the water gets really dirty, you may have to refill the bucket.

If your floor is waxed or no-wax vinyl or linoleum, use a specially formulated cleaner such as Mop and Glo. Rinse your mop, apply a thin line of cleaner to the floor about three feet long, and spread it over the floor with the mop, picking up as much dirt as you can. Sometimes you have to get at stubborn spots on your hands and knees, using a scraper.

Waxing floors. Some people wax floors. I have to admit I never have, but I've read about it and it sounds awful.

If you have linoleum and want to wax it, first use a damp mop to clean it. Then, if it looks dull, you may want to mop it again with a cup of white vinegar in water — the floor will sparkle, they say.

Usually you can get by with just an all-purpose cleaning solution, but once in a while you may have to remove the wax buildup with an all-purpose cleaner or stripper. Always test a spot before stripping to make sure it won't damage the floor. Rinse and apply two thin coats of a self-polishing liquid polish using a long-handled wax applicator.

Best bet: Take out the linoleum and get a no-wax vinyl floor!

Kitchen Tips

To rid the cutting board of garlic or onion smell, cut a lime or lemon in half and rub the surface with the cut side of the fruit. Or make a paste with baking soda and water and apply plenty of it. Rinse off.

If you break an egg on the floor, sprinkle it heavily with salt; after five minutes sweep the dried egg up into the dustpan.

Remove paint spots from glass with hot vinegar.

To remove streaks on stainless steel, rub with baby oil.

Wash your sponge in the dishwasher. The hot water will not only make it look better but also kill the bacteria that like to grow in a moist environment.

Remove food easily by sprinkling the broiler pan, while hot, with dry laundry detergent. Cover with a dampened paper towel and let the burned food set for a while. Food will come off easily.

Loosen grime on the can opener by brushing with an old toothbrush.

Clean the outside of cast-iron pans with a commercial oven cleaner. Let set for two hours and the accumulated black stains can be removed with vinegar and water. After cleaning the pan take a piece of waxed paper and, while the skillet is warm, wipe around the inside to prevent rusting Or rub a little oil on the inside of the pan to keep it seasoned.

To clean copper pots, fill a spray bottle with vinegar and add 3 tablespoons salt. Spray solution liberally on the pot; let set for a while, then simply rub clean. Try toothpaste, Worcestershire sauce, or catsup to polish copper pots. Rub, and tarnish will disappear.

Get rid of bad odors by grinding a lemon half or orange rinds in the garbage disposal.

Rub salad oil on the grater before using for a fast cleanup. Use a toothbrush to brush lemon rind, cheese, onion, or whatever out of the grater before washing.

Scour out coffee and tea stains from plastic cups and dishes with baking soda. If it smells bad, place crumpled-up newspaper in the container; cover tightly and leave overnight.

To clean a thermos bottle, fill it with warm water and a few tablespoons of baking soda, then rinse.

BATHROOMS

It is much easier to live with some dirty rooms than with others. You can easily go to sleep each night knowing there are lots of weird things growing under your bed in the form of dust balls and used tissues, but in the morning when you brush your teeth and wash your face you really need to have a clean sink.

Bathrooms tend to get messy very easily. Towels, makeup bottles, and toothpaste tubes all get thrown around and need to be picked up and put away on a daily basis. Having storage areas or shelves for these items makes it easier to keep the bathroom clean. But even if you have a place for everything, you'll still end up with soap scum.

Rinse out the tub or shower stall after each use. Rinse it while you are still wet. Just spray water on all surfaces, get some soap on a sponge, wipe around the tub or shower, and rinse. The sink should also get this treatment at least once a day.

Keep the tile and porcelain surfaces clean to avoid using abrasives, which scratch surfaces, to get at the built-up gunk.

CLEANER FOR BATHTUBS

Mix ½ cup vinegar with 1 cup clear ammonia and ¼ cup baking soda in a gallon of hot water. Wear rubber gloves and make sure the room is well ventilated (this is strong stuff). Works on fixtures, fiberglass, and porcelain.

You can wait to clean the toilet and floor once a week.
I like to vacuum the floor first to get up all the hair and
loose dirt. Be sure it's completely dry, of course, before
you vacuum.

The Big Clean

When you feel your bathroom needs a big clean,
start with the bathtub.

1. First clean the shower walls around the tub.
   Use a tile cleaner and a tile brush. Tile cleaner needs to sit a while before it works, as it's
   mainly a chemical action that gets things
   clean (directions on the product will tell you
   how long). After it has sat for the proper
   amount of time, start scrubbing the area
   where you first applied it. The brush works
   well because it gets into the grout between
   the tiles. There will be lots of bubbles on the
   wall, making it difficult to determine when
   you have removed all of the grime (you can
   sometimes feel it).

2. If you have a shower door, scrub that, too. If
   the door has a runner, clean it with a toothbrush and a cleaning formula like Fantastik. If
   this doesn't work, use a paint scraper — move
   it back and forth inside the runner. This may
   be rather disgusting the first time you do it,
   but it gets easier each time. Don't rinse anything until you have finished the entire job.

3. The tub can be cleaned after you have taken
   care of the walls and all. If the shower curtain
   is dirty, take it down and put it in the wash or
   throw it out. Use a powdered cleanser on the
   bottom of the tub if your tub can handle it.

Don't use too much of an abrasive at once. If your tub is not porcelain, use a specialty product instead of the powdered cleanser.

4. Use your toothbrush on the tub, starting at the end opposite the faucet. Use that toothbrush at the top of the tub where it meets the tile and all the gook likes to grow. The brush can get out much of this, but you may have to use bleach on some areas. Be sure you do this at the end, though, as bleach can give you a real headache.

5. After you have soaped everything up rinse off everything in the tub. Use your shower head — if it's one of those on a hose, then all the better. If you are thinking about getting a new shower head buy one of these, as it makes cleaning all the easier. Rinse the walls first and then the inside of the tub. Feel the tub to make sure everything has been rinsed off.

6. Clean the sink in the same way, with a little powdered cleanser in the basin. Don't get it on the top of the sink because it's hard to rinse.

Super Solutions for Sinks and Tubs

Use commercial rust removers to remove tough rust stains. Wear rubber gloves with these, though.

Clean discolored porcelain with this solution: Mix cream of tartar with hydrogen peroxide to make a paste. Or mix lemon juice and borax. Scrub the paste into the stain and rinse well.

Is the tub yellowed? Rub it with a small amount of salt and turpentine, mixed to a paste. Rinse well.

Clean grout between tiles by using a toothbrush or nailbrush to clean difficult areas. Dip the brush in bleach to get at difficult spots of mildew.

A cleaner for grout. Mix 3 cups baking soda with 1 cup warm water to a paste. Scrub on grout and rinse off well.

Toilets

Cleaning the toilet has got to be up there on everyone's list of "jobs I wish I didn't have to do." My motto is "Do it fast."

I have found that those cleaners you hang in your toilet do little more than color the water and are no substitute for scrubbing, unfortunately.

Toilets are usually made of vitreous china, which is easy to clean. Be careful when using toilet-cleaning products: Read the directions and don't mix products willy-nilly, so they can produce dangerous fumes when mixed together.

You can clean the toilet with a powdered cleanser:

1. Sprinkle it inside and around the edges of the bowl. Wet a long-handled brush inside the bowl and sprinkle cleanser on it.
2. Starting on the inside upper rim, work the brush in a circular motion, cleaning as deep into the bowl as possible. Be sure to get under the rim and be sure to get all spots.
3. Flush the toilet to rinse.

The outside of the toilet can be cleaned with a liquid cleaner:

1. Put the seat up and clean underneath the seat. Spray the top of the seat, the underside of the lid, and the top of the lid.

2. While the surface is wet, use your toothbrush around all those rubber bumpers and hinges and wipe clean. Also use your brush around those little plastic caps near the floor and around the area where the toilet meets the floor.

3. Use bleach if mildew is growing.

Super Solutions for Toilets

◆ Pour ½ cup chlorine bleach in your toilet bowl and let it stand for ten minutes. Scrub with a brush and flush. This is not recommended for septic tanks, however.

◆ One friend, who used to live on Coca-Cola, said flat cola can clean a toilet bowl. Pour it in and let it stand an hour or so, then scrub and flush.

Mirrors

Use window cleaner on mirrors. Spray it lightly and evenly and wipe with a dry cloth until the glass is dry.

If there is a cloud of hair spray over the mirror, wipe with rubbing alcohol.

To defog a mirror quickly, blow hot air from a hair dryer at it.

Medicine Cabinets

My advice is not to have one of these. Or if you do, don't use it. It's too easy to leave things in them forever. You can find antiques in most medicine cabinets.

Attack them once every few months: Throw out old medicines and cosmetics; wipe and clean the shelves.

Clean the mirror on the outside and any outside shelves weekly, though. Also be sure to clean the toothbrush holder. Put a rag in each hole and run it up and down.

Floors

If your floor is carpeted it will have to be vacuumed; otherwise, you must wash it. Since most bathrooms are small, floors can be washed on your hands and knees.

Starting in a far corner away from the door, use a spray cleaner and some rags. Spray lightly and clean and wipe with cloths, picking up any debris as you go.

Super Solutions for Bathrooms

◆ Use a solution of white vinegar and water to remove hard-water deposits on shower enclosures.

◆ Clean glass shower doors with a sponge and some white vinegar.

◆ Lemon oil will remove water spots on metal frames of shower doors.

◆ Cover spots in grout with white shoe polish.

◆ Use lemon oil on bathroom tiles; it will keep the shine longer and keep water stains from building up quickly. Works on glass shower doors and ceramic tile.

◆ Use rubbing alcohol to shine the chrome faucets on tubs and sinks.

◆ If your shower head is clogged with lime and mineral deposits try boiling it in ½ cup white vinegar mixed with 1 quart water for about fifteen minutes. Plastic shower heads can be soaked in a hot vinegar-and-water solution of the same ratio.

◆ Use a paste of borax mixed with lemon juice on rust stains.

7

MORE ROOMS,
MORE DIRT

*"The art of being wise is the art of knowing
what to overlook."*

— William James

Unfortunately, every room — no matter how little it is used — has to be cleaned eventually. Some are easier than others. Areas that no one uses and those areas where there simply isn't much to clean are easiest. My long entryway just has to be swept. And there's the hall upstairs that just needs to be vacuumed and checked for cobwebs: There's nothing in it to clean. This is one reason why minimalist decorating became so popular.

Sometimes a room becomes a problem area when it is used for too many purposes, however. Disaster strikes when the television room is used for eating, playing, and reading, and remains of everything are strewn from end to end.

It's a good idea to look at a room with a critical eye and figure out what the room is used for — that is, what do people do in the room? Make a list of what goes on in your living room. The results may astound you: There may be everything from reading to telephoning to eating to sleeping going on there. You may find that some of the things on your list may not be suitable for that room, or maybe you would prefer that they not take place in the room at all.

For example, you might take the phone out of the living room and reserve that room for quiet activities. Maybe your children are in the living room rather than the playroom because it is a more attractive place to be. Can you fix the playroom to make it more appealing? Add new lighting or maybe easy-to-reach shelving?

If the room is too crowded, move unneeded items out. Each summer I put away things such as big blankets and pillows to give the room a spare, crisp look. Sometimes if you move things out you realize you can do without them quite well.

BEDROOMS

Bedrooms will be easier to clean if everything that belongs there can be stored away. Under-the-bed storage is a great help for this. Baskets help catch odds and ends — everything from magazines to hair clips. Some headboards have built-in bookcases and shelves where you can store all kinds of things, and a bedside table usually holds all those little treasures with which you can't bear to part. (My theory is that to really know someone you just have to see what they keep in their bedside table. It would amaze you. Just think about your own.)

ATTICS

Attics are killers. I can't get into my attic very easily, so I never use it. In a way this is lucky because it keeps down the amount of junk we save and it's one less space to clean. Of course, if you have an attic it is probably filled with junk (or other treasures). Keep those treasures in neatly labeled boxes and the space will look neater. You may have to dust the place or sweep it once in a while if it gets out of control. Attics don't really have to be all that clean. Only tackle them when you are in the mood to throw things out. Don't go upstairs when you are feeling sentimental — nothing will get done.

BASEMENTS

Basements — I mean real basements, not finished ones — tend to be dark and dank. Some people try to keep them clean, and some are actually immaculate. Again, I'm lucky because my basement is so awful that I never go down there unless I absolutely must. Ours is an old house and the basement is the oldest and scariest part. The spiderwebs are huge, the ceiling is low, and there's a dirt floor. Can you imagine anything worse? I have lived here for eighteen years and I have never even thought about cleaning my basement.

Some jobs just don't seem worth doing.

If you do have a halfway decent basement you may want to clean it, or at least organize it. A big piece of pegboard on the wall will organize all those little things, like jars of nails, tools, and so on. Shelves also work wonders. But to really keep it clean you must be judicious about throwing things out. Too much stuff saved will just lead to a huge mess. Have a tag sale and take the money you make to buy something for the house that you really need. You might also hire somebody to clean out the attic: Often you can find someone to do it for free, if you let them keep some of your stored valuables.

CHILDREN'S ROOMS

If you are to have any hope of keeping children's rooms clean, it's vital that you organize each room so that it's easy for them to learn to put things away. The room usually has to change as the child grows and interests change. A two-year-old may need a low shelf on which to put blocks while a six-year-old may need lots of small boxes in which to put numerous pieces of Legos.

Closets need to fit your children, too. Provide lots of hooks when they're little, and when they can handle hangers be sure they can reach the closet rod. Adjust it as they grow. A basket or hamper near the closest for dirty clothes is a good idea, too.

For more information, see chapter 9, Kids & Pets.

CLEANING YOUR CAR

Whenever you get a new car you say, "I'm going to keep this car clean" — and you really mean it. But before long everything under the sun is in the backseat and the rest is suffering as well.

Vacuum the interior of the car frequently to keep grit out of the carpet. Small cordless vacuums are great for cars. Keep a whisk broom and maybe some paper towels in the car to get at spills when they occur. My coffee spills almost daily, so I have what I call a coffee rag to wipe it up. I keep it tucked under the driver's seat for emergencies: great system.

Use a spray foam carpet cleaner in the car when the carpet gets really dirty. Vacuum only when it's fully dry.

Prevent ashes from smoldering by putting an inch of baking soda or gravel in the ashtray. Or don't allow anyone to smoke in the car!

Chrome needs to be polished. This can actually be fun because the result is so good. Polish the chrome after the car has been washed.

Chrome cleaner. Dip a wet sponge into baking soda and rub onto the chrome. Let it sit for about twenty minutes, then rinse and buff dry with a cloth.

Baking soda cleans spatters and traffic grime from windshields, headlights, chrome, and enamel. Wipe with soda and then a damp sponge. Rinse.

Use plastic net bags (the kind that hold onions) to wash windshields that are covered with insects. Rub away and throw out.

Wash your car in the shade. Close all the windows and hose off all the dirt from the roof and the sides of the car. Spray everything, especially the wheels and under the fenders and bumpers.

Use a commercial car shampoo to wash the car. Apply it with a soft sponge or cloth, scrubbing where necessary. Work from the top down. Wash one area at a time, but keep the water running over the entire car to keep the dirt running off. Rinse before suds dry; dry with a soft towel or a chamois to prevent water spots.

Make leather or vinyl upholstery cleaner by using a soapy solution of soap flakes and water. Apply suds to seats with a brush and wipe clean with a wet sponge. Buff dry.

Wipe or spray rubber gaskets on the door with a heavy coating of vegetable oil so the doors won't freeze together.

If your lock is frozen, heat the key with a cigarette lighter. Never force the key; turn it gently.

Place a bag of kitty litter in the trunk just in case you get stuck in ice or snow — it provides great traction. If you are stuck without litter, remove the rubber mats from the car and place them in front of the rear wheels. This might get you out.

Wash windows with a chamois every time you pump gas. Remember the days when the attendant washed your car windows? Wasn't that fabulous? Now we have to do it ourselves, which can be difficult but can give you something to do while you wait for the gas to be pumped.

Use nail polish remover to get rid of bumper stickers. Gently scrape with a razor blade or knife.

Use a soap-filled steel-wool pad to remove rust spots.

Work a matching-colored crayon into paint scratches.

New car? Try using hot vinegar on the price sheets. Scrape gently and continue adding vinegar until the sheet is gone. Or apply salad oil: Let set for a while and scrape.

Keep reading material in the car. You never know when you'll have to wait while picking up your daughter at her piano lesson, and having something to read will help pass the time.

Keep an old pair of shoes in the car so you can go shopping after work even though your feet are tired and killing you.

A container of wet wipes in the car is great to have even if you don't have a baby. They can wipe up all kinds of spills in a hurry.

IN THE GARDEN OR TOOLSHED

In the early winter, do yourself a favor and organize the outdoor tools. I know this sounds like a lot of work, but it helps — your tools will last longer and you won't lose them.

Try putting up a pegboard in the garage. Use hooks to hang the tools.

If you use a pegboard to hang your tools, outline each tool with paint so you'll know just where it goes.

Clean metal parts of spades, shovels, forks, rakes, and hoes with a wire brush, emery cloth, or steel wool. Apply a protective coating of oil with a rag. Floor wax will make the handles look like new.

Set up a time-saver for next season. Fill an old pail with sand; pour in a quart or so of oil and mix a bit. After every use of hoes, rakes, or what have you, push them into the oily sand a few times. They'll emerge shiny and with a film of oil to keep them from rusting.

Use an old rake head as a hanger for hand tools by attaching it to the wall. Use it.

Keep hoses off the garage floor. Drive three spikes into a board so each spike forms one point of a triangle. Cut three short sections of hose from an old, worn-out hose and cover the three spikes with them. Now hang up the hose and it will last longer.

Is the floor of the garage a mess? To remove oil drippings from concrete, soak with mineral spirits for thirty minutes; scrub with a brush as you add more mineral spirits. After scrubbing, absorb the grease with newspaper. Allow concrete to dry, then wash with a solution of 1 cup laundry detergent, 1 cup bleach, and 1 gallon cold water. Repeat until stains are gone.

Or spread several thicknesses of newspaper over the area where the oil has spilled. Saturate the paper with water and press it firmly against the floor. Allow to dry, remove paper, and oil spots should be gone.

To eliminate oil spots, sprinkle the area with sand or kitty litter. It will absorb the oil and you can just sweep up the litter.

Organize the garage as best you can. Use the walls for storage if space is at a premium. Bikes can be hung on hooks.

Save small glass jars for storing nails and screws.

Cover the teeth of a handsaw when not in use with a piece of old garden hose, split open.

To guard the teeth of a circular saw, store the blades in record album covers.

Clean tools by rubbing a small amount of kerosene on the metal parts vigorously with a soap-filled steel-wool pad. Then gather aluminum foil into a ball and rub it on the surface. Wipe away residue with newspaper and coat lightly with olive oil before putting tools away.

CLEANING THE CHARCOAL GRILL

Mix ½ cup of a liquid cleaner with 1 gallon water and pour it into a heavy-duty plastic garbage bag (or plastic garbage can). Immerse the grill in the bag, secure the bag with a twist tie, and allow the grill to soak overnight. The next day, simply brush away the burned-on soil, rinse, and you are ready to barbecue.

(Be careful with kerosene — always remember that it is flammable.)

Paint a band of red, blue, orange, or yellow on the handles of all your tools. This makes them easier to find when you dump them into the garden weeds or need to find one in the shed quickly.

Storing tools. Attach a plastic berry basket to pegboard and put tools like the screwdriver through the mesh.

Tack cloths last longer when stored in an airtight container to keep from drying out.

Coat the blade of the snow shovel with floor wax and the snow will not stick.

Rust preventer. Use this on tools, metal furniture, and the like to prevent rust. Combine ¼ cup lanolin and 1 cup petroleum jelly in a double boiler over low heat. Stir until it melts, remove from the heat, and pour into a jar. Let it cool a bit; use while still warm by letting it dry on the object.

Before starting a messy job, wipe a thin coat of petroleum jelly on your hands. Before going into the garden, rub your fingernails in a cake of soap.

8

BRIGHTER THAN BRIGHT IDEAS FOR THE LAUNDRY

"Soap and education are not as sudden as a massacre, but they are more deadly in the long run."
— Mark Twain

You either like it or you don't. Yes, it's true, some people actually like to do laundry. Isn't that amazing? I have to admit that I don't dislike doing laundry, but I don't find it very exciting, nor do I always understand it.

When I first had to do my own laundry I simply threw everything in together and settled for lots of pink and purple clothing. Now I know to at least separate things into a few piles: whites, darks, mediums, and reds. We always have a separate red wash because my husband seems to have a thing for red socks.

Laundry is one thing that has to be done regularly. If you don't have a washer and dryer, you probably spend time at a Laundromat or hire someone to wash your clothes. But someday you'll have to do it yourself.

ORGANIZING THE EFFORT

Some people like to have a fixed "laundry day" — one day a week when they wash all their clothes. I tend to do the wash every day: I throw a load in before going to work so the washing machine is going at 7 A.M. each day. Usually one of my children remembers that when she gets home from school she should check the washer and throw the stuff in the dryer. It works fairly well, and we don't have to spend all weekend doing the laundry (only half of it).

In one family I know, each person does his or her own laundry. The man of the house washes his clothes, the woman hers, and they share the rest. The child is only six but she's already learning how the machine works. Great idea. In our house we all try to share — it sometimes works and sometimes doesn't.

It is important to remember that members of both sexes can, in fact, do laundry. Also remember that folding it and putting it away is part of the job. Putting away laundry is worse than washing it, I think.

We have a laundry chute on the second floor that sails down to a shelf in the laundry room. Now wouldn't you think this would be fabulous? And that kids would learn to love to throw their dirty clothes down the chute? Wrong. They still throw their clothes all over their rooms and only throw certain items down the chute. So each family member also has a laundry basket. This works somewhat — at least it gets the clean clothes up to the right room.

Organized types have several laundry baskets in the laundry room. They sort clothes into the baskets by type: whites, colors, permanent press, delicates. Good idea, huh? Then you have other baskets to take the clothes back to each person's room.

If you have lots of kids the same size and all their clothes look alike, mark each item with different-colored dots on the label: Use red for Johnny, blue for Peggy Sue, and so on. This works well.

LABELS AND WHAT THEY MEAN

The first thing to know about laundry is what the clothing is made of and how to take care of that particular fabric. Anything labeled *hand wash* should not go into the washer, or it may shrink. Brilliant. Also, anything labeled *dry-clean only* should probably be dry-cleaned. Blends of fibers should be cared for according to the fiber with the highest percentage in the blend. A blend of 60 percent cotton and 40 percent polyester would be cleaned as if it were all cotton.

Labels are supposed to tell it all, but here's what they mean in case you can't quite figure it out.

Block to Dry. Shape the garment to its correct size and shape it while drying.

Cold Wash/Cold Rinse. Use cold water from a faucet or the cold temperature setting on the washing machine.

Cool Iron. Iron item at the lowest setting.

GOING TO THE LAUNDROMAT

Get a tote of some kind to hold all your supplies so once you get to the Laundromat you don't have to buy something else. Take lots of change with you, too. Read and follow instructions on the wall. Find a good Laundromat — a clean one with an attendant on duty.

Damp Wipe. Just wipe with a damp cloth or sponge and add a little bit of a mild detergent. Surface clean only.

Delicate Cycle, or Gentle Cycle. Can be washed in a machine that has this setting; otherwise, you should wash it by hand.

Do Not Iron. Don't iron this or press using any heat.

Dry-Clean Only. Can be dry-cleaned professionally or you can clean it yourself in one of those dry-cleaning machines.

Dry Flat. Lay garment on a flat surface to dry.

Durable Press or Permanent Press Cycle. Use appropriate machine setting. Or use a warm wash, cold rinse, and short spin cycle.

Hand Wash. Launder by hand only with mild detergent; usually can be dry-cleaned as well.

Hand Wash Only. Launder by hand only in mild detergent in lukewarm water. Machine washing or dry-cleaning is not advisable.

Hot Iron. Iron at a hot setting.

Iron Damp. Dampen article before ironing.

Line Dry. Hang damp and allow to dry.

Machine Wash. Wash and dry as usual.

Machine Wash Separately. Machine wash alone or with same colors only to avoid color bleeding.

No Bleach. Do not use any type of bleach.

Professionally Dry-Clean Only. Do not use a self-service machine; have garment cleaned by a professional dry cleaner.

Steam Iron. Use an iron with steam.

Tumble Dry. Can be tumbled in a dryer at recommended heat on label.

Tumble Dry, Remove Promptly. Can be tumbled dry in a dryer at recommended heat, but if your machine doesn't have a cool-down cycle, remove the garment when tumbling stops.

SORTING

The first step is to sort clothes into different categories. It's easiest to sort by color. Put all the whites in one pile, all the light colors in another, and the bright and dark colors in a third. Then separate the dark pile into colorfast and noncolorfast items.

After you separate by color, separate these piles into "really dirty," "moderately dirty," and "not very dirty."

Now you have lots of piles. The trick is to combine these piles in like groups:

- ◆ Put white and light-colored articles that have similar degrees of soil into one pile.
- ◆ Separate white synthetics and wash them with other whites.
- ◆ Separate permanent press, blends, and synthetics from cottons and other natural fiber garments.
- ◆ Keep apart fabrics that produce lint (towels) from those fabrics that attract lint (knits, corduroy).

Checklist — Preparing Clothes for the Wash
- ◆ Close all zippers, hooks, and buttons.
- ◆ Turn pockets inside out.
- ◆ Remove nonwashable decorative items such as pins or buckles.
- ◆ Pretreat stains or spots with prewash spot-and-stain remover.

PRODUCTS

There are all kinds of items designed to make your washing easier. Study the shelves and try them out. Some detergents contain phosphates, which are harmful to the environment because they can promote an overgrowth of algae in water. Some detergents are phosphate-free, but their cleaning power is not effective in hard water so you may have to condition the water or use a water softener.

Always be sure to follow the manufacturer's instructions for the amount of detergent to use with the wash cycle. Measure carefully. You may have to use more if your clothes are very dirty or if you have hard water.

Bleach

Bleach is that wonder cleaner that works with your detergent to make whites whiter, make brights brighter (in some fabrics), and act as a mild disinfectant. Common liquid chlorine bleach is the most effective, but it is harmful to the environment and can't be used on all fabrics. Oxygen bleach is safer for many fabrics, but it is not as strong as chlorine bleach.

If you use chlorine bleach, first test fabrics by mixing 1 tablespoon chlorine bleach in ¼ cup warm water. Apply solution to a spot you won't notice; wait a few minutes and check for a color change. If it doesn't bleed, use according to directions.

Add diluted chlorine bleach to your wash about five minutes after the wash cycle begins or use the automatic bleach dispenser. Hot water improves the bleach's performance.

Fabric Softeners

Fabric softeners add softness and reduce static electricity. You can find them in liquid, sheet, or solid form. Some are used in dryers and some in washing machines. Careful, though — some people are very allergic to these, especially the sheets. Read instructions carefully.

THE MACHINES

Don't overload the washing machine. Mix small and large items in each load for good circulation and distribute the load evenly around the wash basket.

Cycle selection. Select the type of cycle and the length of washing time according to the kind of load you are washing. Follow the guidelines that come with the washer.

The wrong way to do laundry.

Shake out each item before putting it in the dryer to minimize wrinkling and speed drying time. Don't overload the dryer, and try to take items out of the dryer as soon as it stops.

If you sometimes prefer to hang clothes outside to dry, make sure you use clean clothespins. Attach items to the clothesline by their sturdiest edges. Dry white and light items in the sun, but bright-colored items in the shade. Laundry hung on the line usually evokes pleasant memories of a quieter time of life. It also takes more time, unfortunately — something we don't always have.

LAUNDRY HINTS

- Get white socks white again by boiling them in water with a slice of lemon.
- If your chamois shirt is stiff, soak it in warm water to which a spoonful of olive oil has been added.
- Rub suede lightly with an emery board to remove rain spots.
- A white vinegar solution will remove a permanent crease. Sponge the material with the vinegar and press it flat with a warm iron.
- Scorched whites? Sponge with a piece of cotton that has been soaked in peroxide. Or bleach with water and lay it in the sun to dry.
- To remove chewing gum, apply ice to harden the gum and scrape it off. Soften with egg white before laundering. Or place the garment in a plastic bag and put it in the freezer; scrape off. Or sponge with a dry-cleaning solvent.
- Remove knots from a sweater with a fine piece of sandpaper. Or shave the sweater with a razor.

- Don't dry-clean down-filled comforters. Wash them in a washing machine filled with hot water and soap. Rinse well and tumble dry. When thoroughly dry, shake vigorously to fluff up feathers.
- For comforters filled with synthetic fibers, follow the manufacturer's advice.

Stains

Remember that the first rule of stain removal is to get to the stain as soon as possible in order to maximize your chances of removing it.

Alcohol. Rinse in clear, warm water until the stain is gone, then wash as usual. Nonwashable fabrics can be rinsed with clear, warm water and dried well.

Blood. Cover the area with meat tenderizer. Apply warm water to make a paste and wait twenty minutes, then sponge with cool water or soak using a presoak product. Use diluted chlorine bleach if needed.

Chocolate. Sponge stain with cold water; don't use hot water. Then add 2 tablespoons borax to 2 cups warm water and sponge the stain with the solution. Rinse well and wash as usual.

Coffee. Sponge fresh stains with above borax solution. Rinse and wash as usual. Sponge old stains with cold water, then rub well with glycerine. Leave for half an hour and rinse with warm water.

Egg. Soak fabric in a warm solution of biodegradable laundry detergent and water. Wash.

Grass stains. Wash in hot suds when you can, or sponge with denatured alcohol before washing.

Ink. Saturate with hair spray, rub with a clean cloth, and ink should disappear. Repeat if stain stays. For polyesters, rub with alcohol.

Mildew. Wash new stains in hot, soapy water as soon as possible. For bad stains on whites, soak in a solution of one part chlorine bleach to eight parts cold water for ten minutes. Wring out the water and place in a weak solution of cold water and white vinegar to neutralize the bleaching action. Rinse well and wash.

Milk. Rinse in cool water, then wash with cold liquid-detergent suds.

Perspiration. Remove stains in any of the following ways: Sponge with a weak solution of white vinegar and water; sponge with lemon juice; dissolve two aspirins in water and soak the article; or soak the article in a mild solution of liquid detergent.

Red wine. Sprinkle spill immediately with lots of salt. Dunk it in cold water and rub the stain out before washing.

CLEANING FABRICS RIGHT

It's often a mystery how to clean certain kinds of fabrics, especially when you've lost the label or have received a handmade item as a gift. Here are some guidelines.

Chiffon. Hand wash in lukewarm, soapy water. Squeeze gently until clean; rinse well. Lay the garment flat on a large towel and pull into shape. Place another towel on top and roll up. When almost dry, press with a warm iron.

Chintz. Hand wash in lukewarm, soapy water and rinse well. Add 2 teaspoons powdered size to 1 cup boiling water. Make sure the size is completely dissolved, and strain. Dip the garment into the solution and squeeze out the excess. Roll the garment in a towel to dry partially, then press lightly with a warm iron.

Stiff, hot starch can be used if size is not available. Never use washing soda to wash chintz.

Comforters. Wash down-filled comforters individually in the washing machine with hot water and soap. Rinse well and tumble dry. When dry, shake vigorously to fluff out the feathers.

Do not dry-clean down-filled comforters. (Mine fell apart.)

Cotton. Wash white cotton in hot, soapy water. Mild chlorine bleach can be added to the wash if needed. Rinse well in clean water and wring or spin dry. Press with a hot iron while damp.

Colored cottons can be washed together so long as the colors are fast. Add salt to the water to prevent the colors from running and wash as above.

Wash drip-dry cottons in plenty of hot water. Do not squeeze. When clean, hang up and pull the garment into shape and leave it to drip dry.

Lace. Handle lace with care. Always squeeze the fabric when washing; never rub it. Wash white lace in pure soap flakes and hot water mixed to a thick lather. Pour the soap solution into a jar and add the lace, then cover the jar and shake it for five minutes. Change the soap and repeat the process until the lace is clean. Rinse well in warm, then cold, water.

Next, dissolve 1 teaspoon gum arabic starch in 2 cups water and dip the lace into it. Squeeze out the excess water and roll in a thick towel. Lay the lace flat, facedown on a damp ironing board. Cover with a damp cloth and press with a cool iron.

To freshen black lace, dissolve a few drops of ammonia in 2 cups water and gently sponge the lace with the solution until it is damp. Roll the lace in a cloth and leave it for thirty minutes, then press as above.

> ◾ **SOAP** ◾
>
> The earliest mention of the use of soap comes from early Mesopotamia and Egypt. The Mesopotamians mixed the ashes of rushes, oil, and clay to form a kind of all-purpose cleaning abrasive. Egyptians collected a carbonate of soda from the surface of the earth and used it to clean their clothing and weapons.
>
> The Romans built soap factories, one of which was discovered in the ruins of Pompeii. After the fall of the Roman Empire, housekeeping and personal cleanliness declined.
>
> In the Middle Ages, baths were taken only as a medical prescription and didn't have to involve the use of soap. Dwellings didn't fare much better. In the castles, maids did wash down the benches and tables but simply hid the refuse and filth on the floors under a layer of rushes.
>
> Unfortunately, the unsanitary conditions of the Middle Ages were cited as one factor behind the Black Plague. After the Black Plague, housekeeping came more into vogue. Renaissance homes were cleaner — they started to change those floor rushes.

Do not wash black lace. Store valuable lace in blue tissue paper to preserve its color.

Linen. White linen sheets, napkins, and cloths can be washed like white cotton. Natural-colored linen needs a gentler treatment: Wash in cooler water and do not bleach. Wash dyed linen carefully, squeezing the fabric as little as possible. Press all linens while damp with a fairly hot iron.

Satin. Add ½ tablespoon kerosene to every quart of warm, soapy water needed to immerse the article. Lift the garment up and down in the mixture until clean. Rinse several times in clean, warm water and add a little borax to the final rinse to restore the gloss. Squeeze out the excess water and partially dry, then press on the "wrong" side with a warm iron.

Wool. Avoid extremes of temperature, as woolens will shrink. Do not soak woolens or leave them wet. Do not rub, twist, or wring the fabric. Do not use too much soap, and always rinse well.

Don't machine wash unless specifically approved on the item. Wash wool in hand-hot water in pure soap flakes. Dissolve the soap completely before adding the garment. Agitate gently and repeat in clean suds; rinse in warm water.

You may also wash woolens in cold water with Woolite.

9

KIDS & PETS: YOUR BIGGEST CHALLENGES

"The most important thing that parents can teach their children is how to get along without them."
— Frank A. Clark

If anyone really thought about the mess that pets and kids create, they'd never allow them to live in the house. I mean, kids are basically great, but boy are they dirty. You can tell them a million different times to wipe their feet, and in their excitement over the new dirt pile they've discovered they will forget to do just that. And pets? Try catching a dog that has just been in the river and trying to towel him down before he hits your just-washed floor. It is a rarity indeed.

In the country we have a long mud season. It comes in between winter and spring and is a lot longer than the latter. Mud season is known to drive people crazy: There's this mud in the driveway, in the yard, on the playground — in short, all over. It works its way into the house, creating messes where messes never existed before. And if you have kids or pets, mud becomes a big part of your life.

During mud season, clean floors become an impossibility. I have learned to abandon this idea for a while if I am to remain sane. If you have been blessed with children or animals, don't worry so much about your house; enjoy the little boppers instead.

KIDS

Cleaning the kids isn't always the easiest thing to do. They go through stages: First they love the bath and

When you have kids or pets, a clean house can never be assured.

won't get out of it; then they hate the bath and won't go near it. Next they won't shower for a week at a time; then they won't get out of the shower. Then they are gone.

Cleaning Up After Them

◆ Use an infant seat for bathing a baby in the bathtub, or one of those rubber tubes specially designed for infants. If you use a seat, take out the pad and put a big towel in its place. Place baby in the seat and run water in the tub — you don't need much.

◆ Children who aren't big enough to be alone in the tub might do well in a rubber laundry basket set in the middle of the tub.

◆ Little ones sometimes like to bathe with a diving mask on. This works great for shampooing.

◆ If you have a little one, make sure your house is childproof and it will be easier to clean, too. Keep surfaces clean and free of objects that can be pulled over heads or go into mouths. Keep light cords wrapped or taped tightly around a table leg — this will prevent a crawler from pulling a lamp onto the floor. Use transparent tape so it won't mar the furniture.

◆ The old gum-out-of-the-hair trick: Rub ordinary cold cream into the hair and pull down on the hair several times with a dry towel. Or try rubbing in peanut butter and massage gum and peanut butter between your fingers until gum comes loose. Remove with a tissue. Or freeze the hair with ice cubes and peel off the gum.

Getting Them to Clean Up After Themselves

Children create quite a bit of havoc, and though they add more work they can eventually help out around the house. They can learn to organize at a young age and they can also learn that items must be treated with respect. Maybe parents need to buy fewer toys and to teach children that the toys they own are special and need to be cared for properly.

Make sure children's rooms fit them well. Put hooks at eye level and put the clothes rod low in the closet to make it easy to hang up clothes.

Putting a clothes hamper in or near the closet can teach children to put dirty clothes there as soon as they undress.

Play areas are important. Be sure the play area is in a room that the child likes and put it in a place where the child will want to be — a sunny corner, for example.

Create one spot in the room where toys may be left out for a while — say, a castle made of blocks or a puzzle or a set of Legos that is becoming a cityscape.

Put toys away at the end of each day. Keep toys in color-coordinated containers or in large boxes — all toy animals in one box, all blocks in another, crayons and art supplies in another. Remember, big toy chests or baskets don't work well — everything falls out and gets lost in the bottom, and it's a general mess in itself. Low shelves work much better.

Sometimes charts help with chores. Give a young child a simple chart with a few easy chores to do: Put away shoes, put away toys, pick up clothes, hang up coat. Pictures of these items can go on the chart with a place for a star. Be sure to follow through if you start this and award a star if the little bopper picks up his or her clothes in the morning. Older children can feed the dog, set the table, water plants, clean the cat box, make beds, dust, or vacuum.

THE LAST WORD — FROM MY DAUGHTER (AGE 12)

Any child in his or her right mind hates cleaning. I know — I am one. You (as a parent) may have tried many ways to get your child to at least straighten out his or her room. But really, about an hour after the clothes have been picked up, are they on the floor again? If so, here are some of my helpful hints.

The standard way for making kids clean their rooms is to say: "If you don't clean your room you can't go to your friend's house, watch television, go out for ice cream, and so on."

At my friend's house the procedure is different. She has an entire file just for chores, with about six lists of chores to do daily and weekly — and she and her sisters and her mother actually do them. It's great — it's so organized.

Another thing to try is a chore list, with the days of the week on the side and on the top, a column of the different chores that need to get done. Each time your child does a chore he or she gets a sticker or a star, and at the end of a week a reward is given.

So what method works best? The threat method or the list method? You can experiment with both, but for me, being a victim of both, I prefer the stuff-your-clothes-in-the-closet-and-see-if-you-can-get-away-with-it method.

On rainy days everyone might be assigned a task. Dad may clean the laundry room; Mom may get the hall closet; the kids may each get a room of their choice.

A Little Inspiration

Kids can clean beautifully when they are so inspired. Here are a few tips for inspiring them to do their best:

- Whenever possible, allow children to choose their own favorite tasks. They'll respond better if they are doing things they enjoy, and may become real pros at what they're doing.
- Be sure to thank and praise the child who has done a good job cleaning.
- Make a game out of quick cleanup efforts. Play the kids' favorite music and make a dance of it. Or play a musical-chairs-like game: Each child's task must be done by the time the song is done.
- Rotate tasks so that no child is stuck doing a task he or she hates each time. Perhaps you might write different chores on slips of paper and have children pull them out of a hat.

PETS

Pets are wonderful but they do rule your life if you aren't careful. Teach them early who is boss. Training takes time — be gentle yet firm. Unless it's a cat, and then it will train you.

Some pets are easier to deal with than others. Cats are clean but their litter box is annoying, and they do shed. Poodles don't shed, and some dogs are cleaner than others. Fish are okay but their aquarium can get green and yucky, and birds can be messy (even little ones have a habit of getting their food all over the floor). Turtles are probably the way to go, but they're hard to find these days.

Dogs and Cats

If your new puppy chews on the furniture, put some oil of cloves on the wood. The odor and the bitter taste should keep him away.

Give puppies lots of things they *can* chew on to prevent them from eating all the valuable things in the house. Give them an old stuffed animal or a thoroughly washed-out plastic bottle to chew on. Save old socks and bundle them up into a great toy.

Dogs do make mistakes. If yours does, blot up as much of the moisture as you can, then rub with a solution of vinegar or lemon juice and warm, sudsy water. Blot and blot again. Place a towel over the stain and put a heavy book on top of it. If the towel becomes soggy, replace it with a dry one.

If your cat makes a mistake, follow the same method as above, but once the spot has dried rub it with a cloth dampened in ammonia. This will not only take the odor away but also prevent the cat from ever doing it in that spot again.

If you need to clean your dog in a hurry, try rubbing baking soda into his coat and then brushing him well.

Washing the dog. Add vinegar or lemon juice to the final rinse water. This takes away soap odors. Try putting a tea strainer in the tub drain if your dog is shedding, to save the plumbing. Try a conditioner on dogs with tangled hair.

Remove burrs by working oil into the tangle or by crushing the burrs with pliers. Crushed burrs do not hold on as well and can be more easily brushed or combed out.

Brushes. If the dog's wire brush gets full of hair, clean it with a toothpick. Weave the toothpick back and forth through the wire rows and the hair will loosen up.

Skunk odor. If a skunk has mixed it up with your animal, wash the pet down with tomato juice before washing with shampoo and water. Rinse with a gallon of water to which a few tablespoons of ammonia have been added. Rinse thoroughly with warm water. Another solution that works is vinegar and water: Wash with clear water and follow with a dousing of vinegar and water.

BUGS

Feed your animal yeast powder — or tablets — with his food every day, starting in February and continuing right on through flea season. It's available at health food stores. For some reason fleas don't like to bite dogs — or cats — that have the smell of yeast powder on them.

Fleas are horrible. You may have to bomb your house, vacuum every day, and keep bathing the animals in flea baths. It's a lot of work, and the fleas seem to live forever.

Ants are no fun either. They don't like tansy, so if you can find some, spread it where they are entering the house.

Silverfish? Sprinkle some boric acid mixed with sugar on affected areas.

Roaches? Good luck. See page 117 for some advice.

If stray dogs keep coming to your garbage cans, try sprinkling full-strength ammonia on top of the garbage bags.

If your dog keeps turning over the water dish while tied up outside, try this: Put a stake in the ground and put the water in a large angel food cake pan — over the stake. This should do the trick.

To keep kitty off of your chair or sofa, try putting some mothballs in the cushions. Or, if you have to, cover the area with plastic. Provide other areas for your cat — a soft cushion in a sunny window is perfect.

If you use canned pet food, try opening both ends of the can and pushing the food out. It makes for less mess than the usual scrape-out method.

Pet food. Use an empty cottage cheese container for a cat dish and put leftovers in the fridge with the lid on.

Store the opened pet food can in an old coffee can in the refrigerator to eliminate odors.

Keep pets' dishes on a piece of foam rubber on the floor so they won't slide around.

Sweep up cat hairs with a damp broom before vacuuming. Use a damp sponge or broom on chairs or sofas to get cat hair up.

Shedding. Start vacuuming puppies or kittens gently when they are little and you can do it throughout their lives. Helps with shedding.

Other Pets

Birdcages. Put a large strip of nylon netting around the birdcage. Wrap it around the cage from the bottom up, about twelve to fifteen inches in width, and the seed should stay inside the cage. Only fill the dish half full at first, then watch to make sure the bird has enough to eat.

Perches. Clean the perch in a birdcage by taking it outside and hosing it down, or rub it clean with a scrub brush.

If the bird gets out of the cage, throw a lightweight towel over him and carefully pick him up and put him back.

Hamsters. Has your hamster escaped? Make a hole in the lid of a box large enough to hold the little bugger. Place a paper towel over the hole and put some food on the towel. When he's hungry he'll go for the food, and when he steps on the towel he'll drop into the box.

Fish tanks. If you have a crust on your fish tank, scrub it with nylon netting and vinegar after emptying. Rinse well before putting the fish back.

10

ODDS & ENDS:
MORE TIPS FOR GETTING
THINGS CLEAN

*"Housekeeping consists of a constant
stream of small problems."*
— Eleanor Howe, *Household
Hints for Homemakers*

Tips are those things that everyone always passes along
to you, but if you don't use them often enough they slip
away into the big oblivion in the sky. I know club soda
takes out stains, but I don't know what stains. How
people remember what cleans what amazes me. There
are entire books devoted to stain removal. I am not
going to try to touch on them all here; instead, I'll give
you a gleaning of hints, some for removing stains, others for how to clean hard-to-clean items, and others to
simply make life a bit easier. And isn't that what it's all
about, really?

FURNITURE CARE

Walnut. Rub a scratch with the meat of a fresh, unsalt-
ed walnut.

Mahogany. Rub with a dark brown crayon.

Water marks. To remove a spot rub with a damp cloth sprinkled with a few drops of ammonia. Or apply a paste of butter or mayonnaise and cigarette ashes and buff with a damp cloth. You might also apply toothpaste on a damp cloth to the spots, or try table salt mixed with a light oil.

Candle wax. To remove from wood, soften wax with a hair dryer, wipe with paper towels, and wash with a solution of vinegar and water.

Stickers. Remove from wood by painting with white vinegar. Give it time to soak in, then scrape off gently. Mayonnaise or vegetable oil will also work.

Lint, dust, and pet hair. These can be removed from upholstered furniture by lightly applying a damp sponge.

Rust. Rubbing turpentine on metal furniture will take rust off.

Cigarette burn on furniture? Dip a cotton swab in clear fingernail polish remover and rub it over the burn carefully. If the burn remains, scrape it gently with a dull knife until the discoloration is gone. Paint the depression with clear fingernail polish, then apply a thin layer and let it dry, and repeat until depression is filled. Cover with furniture polish.

CARPETS

Stains. Use plain club soda on fresh stains. Pour some on the spot and let it set for a few seconds, then sponge up. Older stains may need more work: Try combining 2 tablespoons detergent, 3 tablespoons vinegar, and 1 quart warm water. Work this into the stain and blot dry.

Or make a mixture of powdered laundry detergent and warm water and brush it into the stain with a soft brush. Blot up. Repeat if needed.

Burn in carpet. Remove some fuzz from an inconspicuous place in the carpet, either by shaving or by pulling with pliers or tweezers. Roll it into the shape of the burn. Apply a good glue to the backing of the rug and press the fuzz down into the burned spot. Cover with a piece of tissue and place a book on top (this will let the glue dry slowly).

Flattened carpet. Raise pile with a steam iron. Build up good steam and hold the iron over the damaged spot. Do not touch the carpet with the iron. Brush.

Fixing braided rugs. Use clean fabric glue to fix these instead of sewing. It's easy.

Indoor/outdoor carpeting. To remove spots, spray with a commercial prewash spray and let it set for a few minutes, then hose down.

Candle wax. Use your iron to lift candle drips from a carpet. Place a brown paper bag over the spot and put a hot iron over it. The wax will be absorbed into the bag.

Muddy footprints. Sprinkle salt on the carpet and let it stand for an hour before you vacuum. This brightens the carpet as well as lifting muddy footprints.

Gum. Press ice cubes against the gum until it becomes brittle and breaks off. Then use a spot remover to get rid of all of it.

FLOORS

Scratches. Rub away scratches on wood floors with fine steel wool dipped in floor wax.

Heel marks. Wipe off with turpentine or try a pencil eraser.

Polish. Did you know that you can polish woodwork or varnished floors with cold tea?

Mopping. Try mopping with some waxed paper under the mop. Dirt sticks to it and the floor gets shiny. Or put an old nylon stocking over the mop for dusting. Throw the stocking out, and you still have a clean mop.

ODD LOTS

Avoid extra nail holes. To prevent walls from being marked with nail holes from false starts when hanging a picture, make a paper pattern of the picture. After you have found the correct position for the hanger, perforate paper with a sharp pencil to mark the wall. A wet fingerprint will also mark the right spot for a hanger.

Lime deposits. To remove built-up lime from a teakettle, boil a strong vinegar solution (½ cup vinegar to 1 pint water) in the teakettle.

Piano tips. Ivory keys can be cleaned with a soft cloth dipped in alcohol or lemon juice. Wipe clean with a damp cloth. To *prevent* ivory keys from yellowing, keep them exposed to sunlight. Put a cork at each end of the keyboard — if the lid drops, fingers will be spared.

Drinking glasses. If glasses stick together, fill the top glass with cold water and set the bottom one in hot water to separate them.

Candleholders. To remove wax coated on the holders, place them in the freezer for an hour or so. The wax will peel off.

Prevent candle drips. Put candles in the freezer before you burn them — they won't drip as much.

The joy of stain removal is in its often magical results.

Ballpoint ink stains. Sponge with sour milk. Or saturate with hair spray. Allow to dry. Brush with solution of water and vinegar, and blot excess.

Cleaning combs and brushes. Add about 3 tablespoons baking soda and the same amount of bleach to a basin of warm water. Put brushes and combs in and mix them around; rinse and drip dry.

Eyeglasses. Try a drop of vinegar or vodka on each lens to get them clean.

Jewelry. Clean with a soft cloth dabbed in toothpaste.

Old radiators. If you have one of those big, old-fashioned radiators, try hanging a damp cloth behind it and blowing it with the blower end of the vacuum cleaner. Dust and dirt will be blown into the damp cloth.

Telephone. Clean with rubbing alcohol.

Pewter. Rub with cabbage leaves to clean.

Polish pewter by adding olive oil to a mild abrasive.

Silver. Prepare silver-polishing cloths by mixing 1 cup water with silver paste, and soak clean towels in mixture. When saturated, hang cloths to dry without squeezing. Use these to dry silver after washing.

Prevent silver from tarnishing by washing soon after use. Many foods contain ingredients like salt and acids that lead to tarnish.

Wicker is all the rage right now. To keep it from turning yellow, wash with a solution of warm salt water. To prevent it from drying out, apply lemon oil occasionally. Never let it freeze, as it will crack and split. It likes to be kept moist, so you may need a humidifier in the winter if your house is dry.

Sponges and loofahs. Soak in a strong solution of vinegar and water for twenty-four hours to get rid of sour odors. Rinse several times in cold water and dry outside.

To revive an old silk umbrella, dissolve 1 tablespoon sugar in 1 cup boiling water. Open the umbrella and sponge the silk with the sugar solution, segment by segment, from the shaft to the tips. Hang the umbrella to dry.

To prevent scale buildup in whirlpool tubs, add 3 tablespoons dishwasher detergent to the whirlpool once a week. Let the pump run a few minutes and drain. This will also help keep the pump in good working order.

Wallpaper is hard to remove. You can rent a steamer, but it takes a lot of time. You can also use equal parts of vinegar and hot water. Wet the paper thoroughly with this and after two applications the paper should peel off.

A WORD ABOUT ROACHES

Roaches are the worst — it can be very difficult to get rid of them. They come inside for food and water, remember, so remove the source and half the war is won. You also must destroy any and all roach eggs (they are brown and about the size of a grain of rice).

Roaches like any dark place, so vacuum under the refrigerator, under the heater, under the furniture, under the sink (pipes, too), under stove burners, behind the toilet, behind the piano, under the washing machine, in the folds of drapes, behind books, behind the heavy dresser — all the hardest places to get at, in other words.

After eggs have been destroyed, spray with one of those horrible roach sprays, or try turpentine. A mixture of two parts borax and one part sugar can also be used. Spread this around wherever roaches might be. It's nonpoisonous but slow. And if any water, food, or garbage is available to them, the roaches won't feed on the borax, so put everything in sealed containers. And be sure to put away the dog or cat dish.

Crayon. If your child has decided to color the walls, treat the marks as grease spots. Rub lightly with a dry, soap-filled steel-wool pad, or rub gently with baking soda sprinkled on a damp sponge.

Curtain hooks. Before using, rub them with an oily rag. This prevents rusting and helps protect the curtain from tearing. To clean old hooks, soak them in water with ammonia added. Rinse in clean water and dry.

When mailing cookies to your child at college or camp, pack them in popcorn to keep them from crumbling.

Flies. Hang clusters of cloves in each room to keep them away.

Tree needles from Christmas trees. Hold a panty hose to the nozzle of a vacuum and allow the vacuum to suck in both the hose and the needles. When finished, pull out the panty hose and throw it and the needles away. You will not have to worry about a plugged vacuum again.

STORAGE HINTS

Store out-of-season clothes in large, plastic, lidded trash cans. They'll stay mothproof and dry, even in a damp basement.

When storing china plates, insert paper napkins between each one to prevent scratching.

Preserve silver by wrapping in an acidproof material — not in newspaper or in drawers of oak cabinets.

Saving newspaper clippings. Want to save that great article about your child's art award? Dissolve a milk of magnesia tablet in a quart of club soda overnight. Pour the solution into a pan large enough to hold the flattened paper. Soak for one hour, remove, and pat dry. Do not move until all dry. This, said my favorite librarian and town historian, really works.

If postage stamps are stuck together, put them in the freezer. They will usually come apart and will still be usable.

Storing plastic wrap. My aunt keeps it in the refrigerator because this keeps it from sticking together.

GETTING RID OF ODORS

New paint. To get rid of the smell, place a handful of hay in a bucket of warm water and leave it in the room overnight.

Cabbage or cauliflower cooking odors can be prevented by adding a little lemon juice to the water.

Fish and onions. Add lemon skins to the dishwasher to eliminate the smell.

To get musty odors out of a trunk, place a coffee can filled with kitty litter deodorizer inside the trunk overnight.

USING THE RIGHT STUFF

Not everything is as simple as it seems. A tub is not a tub anymore, and you have to be careful about what type of cleanser you use on the type of surface your appliance happens to have. There's a whole new world of acrylics, laminates, and vinyls, all designed to look shiny and require a minimum of care through years of normal use and thorough cleaning with products specially formulated to help protect their high-gloss finishes.

Stainless-steel sinks, shiny laminate counters, and fiberglass tubs and showers can be permanently damaged with one application of the old hard-abrasive cleaners, which rely on silica for scouring power. To help protect the new finishes, manufacturers have switched to calcium carbonate, a gentler abrasive also blended into many toothpastes. Some of these cleansers (such as Comet) also bleach as they clean.

No-wax floors retain their high gloss with a wear layer of polyurethane or polyvinyl chloride, applied by the manufacturer. Harsh cleansers can damage the

QUICK SOLUTIONS

If you don't have what you need at home, try these
substitutions.

Item	Substitute
Toilet bowl cleaner	Full-strength bleach or vinegar (not together)
Cold cream	All-vegetable shortening
Glass cleaner	Alcohol, ammonia, or vinegar
Shampoo	Mild liquid dishwashing detergent diluted with water
Shaving cream	Baby oil
Talcum powder	Cornstarch
Toothpaste	Baking soda plus salt and flavoring

finish and take the shine away. Some liquid cleaners
have been redesigned to work on no-wax floors, leaving
the floor surface shiny. Before buying a new product,
read the label carefully and be sure the product is com-
patible with your surface.

Surfaces Ranked from Hardest to Softest

These surfaces are ranked from hardest to softest.
The hardest ones can take abrasive scouring, but the
softest ones only like liquid cleaners.

1. **Porcelain enamel sinks and tubs.** Hard
   porcelain coating over a metal base, porcelain
   enamel is safe to scrub with any cleanser.

2. **Fiberglass bathing fixtures.** One hundred percent fiberglass is safely cleaned with soft-abrasive cleansers.

3. **Stainless-steel sinks.** The carefully buffed patina can be marred by hard abrasives. Soft-abrasive cleansers won't hurt finish.

4. **Plastic laminate countertops.** Matte finishes are usually safe to scour lightly with a soft-abrasive cleanser. To protect a high-tech gloss laminate, avoid even soft cleansers and stick to liquid cleaners.

5. **Cultured marble sinks.** Made of ground minerals mixed with hard plastics and molded under heat, these surfaces are cleaned safely with soft-abrasive cleansers.

6. **Soft plastic and plastic-coated bathing fixtures.** These include the acrylic tubs, whirlpool baths, and spas, as well as gel-coated polyester fiberglass fixtures, fiberglass-reinforced fixtures, and PVC-coated fixtures. If it looks shiny and plastic coated and you don't have any manufacturer's cleaning recommendations, don't use even a soft-abrasive cleanser. Use a liquid cleaner formulated to remove soap scum, and you should find that the shiny surface will come clean without a scouring powder.

DISPOSAL DOS AND DON'TS

Always read the label of your cleaning products carefully. Substances that are poisonous, corrosive, or flammable — or packages that should not be incinerated or punctured — will be clearly labeled for consumer safety.

It is our responsibility to dispose of products and

materials safely. Here is a list of specific dos and don'ts to follow:

Do buy the right amount of the product for the job you have to do — this avoids waste and needless disposal of harmful chemicals.

Do use up any product you buy. If you can't, give it to someone who can. Make sure that any product you give away is in its original container with its label intact and that all use and disposal instructions are included. Give leftover paint to a local theater group, donate leftover pesticides to the local garden club, and so on.

WORDS OF WARNING

When reading the label of a new product, look for these words:

Caustic products such as oven cleaners will chemically burn the skin. Avoid splashing; wear safety goggles and rubber gloves.

Poisonous household cleaning products usually cause nausea, vomiting, or diarrhea if ingested. Call a poison-control center or emergency room. Be sure you know where to find this number immediately if you have small children.

Toxic Fumes from products dictate that you work outside or in a well-ventilated room. If this is not possible, step outside often while working.

Flammable products require that you do not smoke or use them near heat, sparks, or flames. Be sure the pilot light is out when working near a gas stove or water heater.

Do recycle wastes if you can. Take used or contaminated motor oil, transmission fluid, or diesel fuel to an automotive service center, oil-recycling station, or authorized collection site. Turn in your old car battery.

Do wrap the container in newspaper before placing it in the trash if the label carries a warning about not getting the contents on your skin.

Do dispose of products that go down the drain during normal use by pouring them down the drain with lots of water. Dispose of each product separately, small amounts at a time. This includes sink and drain cleaner, laundry products, soaps, and so on.

Do empty all aerosol cans, by depressing the button until no more product comes out, before putting them in the trash. Never throw empty aerosol containers into an incinerator or trash compactor.

Do follow all label directions.

Don't dispose of any materials by pouring them into your backyard or into a storm sewer.

Don't bury any containers, empty or full, in your backyard.

Don't attempt to use a backyard fireplace or barbecue as an incinerator.

Don't dispose of anything in dumps by the side of the road.

Don't remove product labels.

Don't remove products from their original containers.

Don't refill empty containers, even with the same material, unless the label recommends it. Once a container is empty, dispose of it. Follow label instructions about rinsing the container or wrapping it in newspaper.

The above information, and more if you need it, is available from: The Household Products Disposal Council, 1201 Connecticut Avenue N.W., Suite 300, Washington DC 20036; (202) 659-5535.

OTHER SAFETY TIPS TO REMEMBER

◆ Keep all cleaning agents out of the reach of children. Sweet-smelling and colorful mixtures can be especially tempting.

◆ Never store cleaners near any heating element.

◆ Unless specifically instructed by the manufacturer, never mix household cleaners. Mixing chlorine bleach with acids produces chlorine gas; mixing it with such alkaline cleaners as ammonia produces chlorine and other noxious gasses. The fumes can be lethal.

◆ If you follow a cleanser with a rubdown of bleach, rinse the surface thoroughly with water first and use each product separately. Rinse after bleaching as well.

◆ Remove any automatic cleaners when cleaning the toilet with another product. Flush several times before using another cleaner.

11

HIRING SOMEONE TO HELP

"You do not want a maid if you don't
feel at all put upon by the job of housekeeping.
Otherwise, if you're still breathing, you probably do."
— Carol G. Eisen, *Nobody Said*
You Had to Eat off the Floor

Let's face it: Most of us are too busy to clean. And in order to have some time to ourselves when we're not working it often pays to hire someone to clean our houses for us or at least do those jobs that we hate to do.

Hiring a cleaning person isn't the easiest job in the world. It takes time to find someone who is reliable and who can clean, too. I once had a fabulous cleaning man. He whipped around the entire house in two hours, and he cleaned everything. His only problem was that he usually broke at least one thing each time he cleaned because of his speed. This got to be expensive.

Another time I had a cleaning couple. They worked as a pair — one vacuumed while the other scrubbed, and the like. They were great. Unfortunately, they went to better jobs and left cleaning behind. This is a problem with many cleaning people: They don't like to clean any more than we do.

FINDING A HOUSEKEEPER

The best way to find a good cleaning person is to ask your friends. Usually, if they have a great one they won't tell you. But sometimes theirs has a relative or friend who is looking for work. It's better to go through someone you know, I have found, than to pick a name out of a hat. Going through a professional cleaning service can work fairly well, though. Lots of times these services work in teams and clean your house fast — usually quite well, too.

HIRING

When you meet your cleaning person for the first time, be specific about what you want done and how you want it done. Most cleaning people do not come with their own supplies, so you need to have these there for them. Sometimes cleaning people will like a certain kind of mop; if so, invest in it and figure that they will be using it more than you will.

Find out what the charge will be (most charge by the hour), and either specify a certain number of hours you want them for or let them figure it out by the size of the house and what you want done. Shop around and compare prices around your area for comparable work.

Once you have found someone you want to try, hire that person on a trial basis to see how it goes. If all goes well, sign him or her on for life. A person who likes to clean and does it well is hard to find.

Remember that. And treat your cleaning person with kindness. If he or she likes a beer at the end of the day, make sure you have a beer in the refrigerator. At Christmas give him or her a nice bonus.

My cleaning person only comes once a week (when she remembers), but people with a higher standard of cleanliness may like someone more than once a week. You'll have to see what you like cleaned and what you can afford. Hiring someone isn't cheap, but to me it's a necessity. It makes for a more harmonious home life. And I'll pay anything for that.

Hiring a Cleaning Service

Professional cleaning services are booming. Over the last few years, franchised maid services nationwide have doubled in number from 812 to more than 1,600, according to ServiceMaster MLP. ServiceMaster is an industrial cleaning company that controls Merry Maids, the largest maid service in the United States with 400 franchises in 45 states and Great Britain. Nationwide, there are 7,200 franchised and nonfranchised home-cleaning services.

Again, the best way to choose a home-cleaning service, like choosing an individual, is to ask friends for references. Then check with your local consumer affairs department to see if it has received any complaints about the service. If not, great.

Ask the service these questions:

- Are your employees bonded?
- Are you insured?
- Do you guarantee your work?
- Do you provide cleaning supplies?
- Who will be responsible for paying the workers' Social Security and taxes?

Before letting a group of strangers into your home, find out if they have insurance so if that prized vase is broken, you are covered. Some have no insurance, while others will cover damage that results from accidents or negligence.

Rates can vary widely. Sometimes they charge one rate for light housework and a higher hourly rate for heavier work like washing walls. You usually must pay for a minimum of four hours. For some work, like washing windows, there is a fixed rate. Check the services' schedules. Some will work conventional hours and others will match your needs.

The level of expertise among services can also vary, so see if the company trains its employees. If you have expensive furnishings, be sure you check on the skill of the workers.

Once you have hired a company, tell them exactly what you want done. If there are several workers, be sure to provide a room-by-room list of tasks to be done.

If you find a good housekeeper, treat her like a queen.

Check the work that same day. It is easier to redo the work then instead of having them return the next day to get it right (they may charge you again, too).

INVENT A MAID

One clever bachelor I know says he has the answer to the dirty apartment dilemma: He has invented a maid. He simply pretends to have a maid, but one who doesn't do a very good job. When people come over for a beer he mentions that "Evelyn" didn't show up today, or that she showed up but didn't get past the study.

"What can I say? She's having a hard time and just didn't get to it all," he moans as he picks up his shirt and kicks a dust ball under the sofa.

He even has a woman's tattered sweater hanging on the coat tree, and he says she must have forgotten it.

He is deadly serious about this and says it has worked . . . so far.

REASONS TO FIRE A CLEANING PERSON

1. Unreliable; shows up late about half the time and leaves early.
2. Does not clean well, even though you leave lots of instructions and offer several chances to get it together.
3. You find that all of a sudden you are missing small things.
4. You constantly hear his or her tales of woe and you don't want to get involved.

When you fire an individual who is not part of a service, give some type of severance pay. Write a reference, if deserved.

$\diamond \diamond \diamond$ **12** $\diamond \diamond \diamond$

SOME CLOSING THOUGHTS

"Many successful executives, artists, scientists and homemakers are messy — and their messiness is part of their success."
— Dr. Danilo Ponce, psychiatrist,
University of Hawaii

When I read the above in a newspaper article I was thrilled. Dr. Ponce went on to say that messiness and success go together in the following ways:

- Creativity arises from a messy environment. Ideas come from places we seldom expect.
- Accepting a certain amount of messiness gives you more time for real work. Some people spend so much time being organized that they don't accomplish much.
- Being messy can help you be flexible and open to new ideas.
- Messiness can help you be more socially success-ful. If you relax and appear less rigid, those around you will be more comfortable.
- If you are messy, you may worry less.

◆ Messiness may help your love life. If you can tolerate some mess, you won't expect your loved ones to be perfect.

Isn't that great news? We who are just a little bit messy can relax. We are probably going to live longer, be calmer, and have lots of lovers — or something like that. I think you can be messy and also be clean. And if you can do that, though you may need some help at it, you have got it made.

Just remember: Save your old toothbrush for the fine cleaning work and always keep some baking soda around — it cleans everything. Throw out anything you think you really don't need, keep the dishes washed, use potpourri in every room so the house at least smells great, and you're halfway there.

The rest depends on you and those around you. One thing about housecleaning: It doesn't go away. So the only way to handle it is to do it as quickly as you can and then do something that you really want to do. Just practice. You'll get better at it, and in the end you'll be happier, too.

APPENDIX

✦ ✦ ✦ ✦ ✦

PRODUCT ASSISTANCE

The U.S. Consumer Product and Safety Commission has a toll-free number, 1-800-638-2772. To obtain information on a commercial product, you can check the product label or ask your local library for the address and telephone number of the manufacturer. Call manufacturers for information about specific products.

POISON INFORMATION

Contact your local poison center about the health effects of products and for information about treating poisoning. The telephone number for poison control usually appears on the inside cover of your telephone directory.

CLEANING WITHOUT CHEMICALS

In recent years we've all heard more and more horror stories about the damaging effects that toxic chemicals can have on our bodies. Yet who is willing to give up blue toilet cleaners that bubble and boil to let us know that they're working? As reluctant as you might be to do away with such wonder products, giving a nontoxic substitute a try has probably occurred to you now and again as something you really *should* do. Well, here's your chance.

The list of substitutes that follows will provide inexpensive alternatives that you can try without spending money on commercial products that might provide disappointing results. One word of warning: When you give up the toxic miracle workers, you will probably have to expend a little more elbow grease to get the same results. So consider your foray into the world of toxin-free cleaning as an extension of your exercise program. Your body will thank you — in more than one way!

Borax

This common household product will help you save storage space and money by using just one simple cleanser in all of the rooms of your house.

Make your own household cleaner for walls and floors by adding ½ cup borax to 2 gallons warm water, ½ teaspoon dishwashing liquid, 1 tablespoon ammonia or simply warm water, and ⅓ cup laundry detergent.

Give diapers and baby clothes a cleaning boost by soaking soiled clothes in ½ cup borax for each diaper pail full of warm water. Follow soaking with a hot water wash, adding ½ cup borax along with the recommended amount of detergent. This will help get rid of odors, reduce staining, and make the diapers more absorbent.

Neutralize pet urine and sour milk odors by dampening the spot and sprinkling borax over it. Rub into areas and let dry. Brush or vacuum to remove the dry borax.

Deodorize your toilet bowl by sprinkling ¼ cup borax and allowing it to stand for at least 30 minutes (overnight is even better). Your toilet bowl brushes can also benefit from an occasional soak in borax.

Wash garbage pails with a solution of borax and warm water to deodorize. You can then sprinkle a little dry borax in the bottom of the dry pail to minimize spoiled food odors as the pail becomes full.

Wash away lingering odors and spilled food in the refrigerator with a sponge or soft cloth using a solution of 1 quart warm water and 1 tablespoon borax. Rinse with cold water.

Brighten porcelain enamel surfaces with a solution of borax and warm water. Sprinkle on a damp sponge or soft cloth and use as you would a powdered cleanser. Rinse thoroughly.

Bring out the shine of fine china without causing fine, hand-painted designs to fade by rinsing china in a sinkful of warm water combined with ½ cup borax. Then give the china a second thorough rinse with clear water.

Care for delicate hand washables by dissolving ¼ cup borax and 1 to 2 tablespoons detergent in a basin of warm water and allowing them to soak for 10 minutes.

Adapted from 20 MULE TEAM Borax: A Guide to Laundry and Household Uses *and used with permission from The Dial Corporation, makers of 20 MULE TEAM Borax.*

Vinegar

Vinegar is very popular these days and there is a simple reason for it — it is a handy, nontoxic cleanser to always have on hand. Other products may cost more or have more elaborate packaging, but few can accomplish the wide variety of tasks that vinegar can.

Remove water rings on wooden furniture by combining vinegar and olive oil in equal parts. On clean soft cloth, work mixture with the grain to erase water rings.

Rejuvenate carpet colors by brushing with a mixture of 1 cup vinegar in 1 gallon water.

Remove mildew from most surfaces by applying vinegar at full strength or mixed with water.

Wash windows and mirrors by mixing 1 tablespoon vinegar in 1 quart water. Apply to the window in the same manner as commercial window-cleaning products.

Clean plastic or vinyl upholstery with a soft cloth dampened with a solution of water and vinegar.

Clean walls, woodwork, and blinds by mixing 1 cup ammonia, ½ cup vinegar, and ¼ cup baking soda in 1 gallon warm water. Apply with sponge or soft cloth and rinse.

Clean your oven by applying vinegar at full strength with a sponge to the doors and walls.

Cut the amount of grease on dishes by adding a capful of vinegar to the dishwater.

Open clogged drains by bringing vinegar to a boil and pouring a small amount down the drain. Let it sit for 5 to 10 minutes, then run hot water. Repeat if necessary.

Remove dried paint on glass by applying heated vinegar to paint on window glass to soften.

Baking Soda

Already mentioned many times, baking soda is a wonderful household alternative because its mildly abrasive quality and its ability to absorb odors make it a versatile cleaning agent.

Brighten white appliances by applying ¼ cup baking soda and 1 quart warm water with a cloth. Rinse after 10 minutes.

Clean your oven by scrubbing with a mixture of baking soda and vinegar.

Soak hard-to-clean pans overnight with a thick layer of baking soda and scrub off the next morning.

Deodorize your freezer, refrigerator, cabinet, or pantry by leaving an open container of baking soda in the area.

Clean the inside of your microwave with a solution of ¼ cup baking soda and 1 quart warm water.

Remove mildew and hard-water stains from your shower by scrubbing with a sponge covered with a baking soda paste.

Clean your toilet by pouring ½ box baking soda into the toilet tank each month. Let the soda set overnight and flush the toilet in the morning.

Eliminate germs and stains on cutting boards by sprinkling baking soda over surface, then pouring vinegar over soda. Once the fizzling has ceased, rinse with hot water.

Remove strong odors such as onion or garlic from porous surfaces by spreading baking soda over surface and then rinsing with warm water.

Freshen your dish towels and sponges by sprinkling baking soda on them after each use.

Lemon Juice

Although lemon juice may not be as versatile as the three household products listed above, it can still be used to brighten and clean your home without the harsh chemicals found in commercial cleansers.

For light cleansing, use the peel from citrus fruits such as lemons and oranges.

Wash windows with lemon juice to leave them streak-free.

Remove mildew by scrubbing with a mixture of lemon juice and salt.

Cut through tough grease with lemon juice applied to a sponge or cloth.

Make your own spray cleanser by mixing 2 tablespoons lemon juice, ½ teaspoon liquid soap, ½ teaspoon washing soda, and 1 teaspoon borax into 2 cups hot water. Mix until dissolved.

Add a nice clean scent as well as cleansing power to all your cleansers by adding lemon juice.

Deodorize your garbage disposal by grinding lemon peels with lots of water.

HOUSEHOLD HAZARDOUS WASTE REFERENCE

SUBSTANCE	PROBLEM
Bleach and liquid cleaners	Contain strong oxidizers. Can cause burns.
Cleansers and powdered cleaners	Contain strong oxidizers. Poisonous. Can cause burns.
Drain cleaners	Poisonous. Can cause serious burns. May contain carcinogens.
Dyes	Poisonous, especially to children; don't use cooking utensils when dyeing. May be carcinogenic.
Furniture polishes	Include various poisonous solvents. One ounce (25 grams) may be lethal to an adult.
Mothballs	Contain poisonous chemical compounds.
Oven cleaners	Poisonous. Can cause serious burns. May contain carcinogens.
Silver polishes	Poisonous. May contain carcinogens. One ounce (25 grams) may be lethal to an adult.
Spot removers	Poisonous. Most are solvent-based. May be carcinogenic.
Toilet cleaners	Spray cans are the most dangerous. Poisonous. Can cause serious burns. One teaspoonful (5 ml) may be lethal to an adult.
Window cleaners	Contain harmful chemical compounds and sometimes carcinogens. May cause birth defects.

PROPER DISPOSAL	ALTERNATIVES
Wash down drain with lots of water.	Use powder, not liquid bleach.
Wrap tightly in plastic, place in a box, tape shut, and put in garbage.	Baking soda and mild detergent, elbow grease.
Wash down drain with lots of water or take to hazardous waste collection site.	Boiling water, plunger, metal snake.
Wrap tightly in plastic, place in a box, tape shut, and put in garbage.	Use vegetable dyes such as onion skins, teas, marigolds.
Use up according to directions or take to hazardous waste collection site.	Mineral oil with lemon oil (but this may strip finish), or Carnauba wax.
Use up according to directions or take to hazardous waste collection site.	Cedar chips, newspapers; wrap wool clothing in plastic bags during warm seasons.
Use up according to directions or take to hazardous-waste collection site.	Salt, quarter cup (60 ml) of ammonia overnight.
Use up according to directions or take to hazardous waste collection site.	Soak silver in water with baking soda, salt, and small piece of aluminum foil.
Use up according to directions or take to hazardous waste collection site.	Immediate cold water and detergent, rubbing alcohol, or a little acetone.
Wash down drain with lots of water.	Mild detergent or small amounts of bleach.
Wrap tightly in plastic, place in a box, tape shut, and put in garbage.	Vinegar and water.

SOURCE: League of Women Voters of Marin County, California. Used with permission. For further information, contact your local solid waste authority.

BIBLIOGRAPHY

✦ ✦ ✦ ✦ ✦

Aslett, Don. *Clutter's Last Stand.* F & W Publications, Inc., 1984.

———. *Stainbuster's Bible.* Penguin, 1990.

Barndt, Herb. *Professor Barndt's On-the-Spot Stain Removal Guide.* Doubleday, 1992.

Barry, Dave. *Dave Barry's Homes and Other Black Holes.* Ballantine Books, Inc., 1995.

Berthold-Bond, Annie. *Clean & Green: The Complete Guide to Non-Toxic & Environmentally Safe Housekeeping.* Ceres Press, 1990.

Campbell, Jeff, and The Clean Team Staff. *Speed Cleaning.* Dell Publishing, 1997.

Chesnut Moore, Alma. *How to Clean Everything.* Simon & Schuster, 1977.

Consumer Guide, ed. *Practical Hints & Tips.* Consumer Guide, 1994.

Eisen, Carol B. *Nobody Said You Had to Eat off the Floor.* David McKay Company, Inc., 1971 (out of print).

Howe, Eleanor. *Household Hints for Homemakers.* D. Appleton Century Co., 1943 (out of print).

O'Rourke, P. J. *Bachelor Home Companion.* Grove Atlantic, Inc., 1997.

Pinkham, Mary Ellen. *Mary Ellen's Best of Helpful Hints.* Warner Books, Inc., 1989.

Proux, Earl. *Yankee Home Hints.* Yankee Books, 1993.

Time-Life Staff. *Cleaning & Stain Removal.* Time-Life, 1990.

Wylie, Harriet. *420 Ways to Clean Everything.* Random House Value Publishing, Inc., 1992.

Winston, Stephanie. *Getting Organized.* Warner Books, 1991.

INDEX

✦ ✦ ✦ ✦ ✦